**REA**

**ACPL ITEM
DISCARDED**

D1121126

JUL 0 8 2009

# DESPERATELY
# WICKED

## PHILOSOPHY, CHRISTIANITY
## AND THE HUMAN HEART

## PATRICK DOWNEY

IVP Academic

An imprint of InterVarsity Press
Downers Grove, Illinois

*InterVarsity Press*
*P.O. Box 1400, Downers Grove, IL 60515-1426*
*World Wide Web: www.ivpress.com*
*E-mail: email@ivpress.com*

©*2009 by Patrick Downey*

*All rights reserved. No part of this book may be reproduced in any form without written permission from InterVarsity Press.*

*InterVarsity Press® is the book-publishing division of InterVarsity Christian Fellowship/USA®, a student movement active on campus at hundreds of universities, colleges and schools of nursing in the United States of America, and a member movement of the International Fellowship of Evangelical Students. For information about local and regional activities, write Public Relations Dept., InterVarsity Christian Fellowship/USA, 6400 Schroeder Rd., P.O. Box 7895, Madison, WI 53707-7895, or visit the IVCF website at <www.intervarsity.org>.*

*The Scripture quotations quoted herein are from the* Revised Standard Version of the Bible, *copyright 1946, 1952, 1971 by the Division of Christian Education of the National Council of the Churches of Christ in the U.S.A. Used by permission. All rights reserved.*

*Design: Cindy Kiple*

*Images: Bust of Plato: Bust of Plato (c. 427-347 B.C.) (stone) (b/w photo) by Greek, Vatican Museums and Galleries, Vatican City, Italy/Alinari/The Bridgeman Art Library*

    *Jeremiah: Time & Life Pictures/Getty Images*

    *Jean-Jacques Rousseau: Jean-Jacques Rousseau (1712-78) (oil on canvas) by Maurice Quentin de la Tour (1704-88) (after), Musee de la Ville de Paris, Musee Carnavalet, Paris, France/Lauros/Giraudon/The Bridgeman Art Library*

    *Thomas Hobbes: Protrait of Thomas Hobbes (1588-1679) engraved by James Posselwhite, Private Collection/The Bridgeman Art Library*

    *Friedrich Wilhelm Nietzsche: Friedrich Wilhelm Nietzsche in 1883, illustration from 'Nietzsche' by Daniel Halevy, Private Collection/The Bridgeman Art Library*

    *Aristotle: The Granger Collection, New York*

*ISBN 978-0-8308-2894-4*

*Printed in the United States of America* ∞

 *InterVarsity Press is committed to protecting the environment and to the responsible use of natural resources. As a member of Green Press Initiative we use recycled paper whenever possible. To learn more about the Green Press Initiative, visit <www.greenpressinitiative.org>.*

**Library of Congress Cataloging-in-Publication Data**

*Downey, Patrick, 1958*
  *Desperately wicked: philosophy, Christianity, and the human heart/*
  *Patrick Downey.*
    *p. cm.*
  *Includes bibliographical references and indexes.*
  *ISBN 978-0-8308-2894-4 (pbk.: alk. paper)*
  *1. Heart—Biblical teaching. I. Title.*
  *BS680.H416D69 2009*
  *233'.5—dc22*

                  *2008046019*

**P**   21   20   19   18   17   16   15   14   13   12   11   10   9   8   7   6   5   4   3   2   1

**Y**   27   26   25   24   23   22   21   20   19   18   17   16   15   14   13   12   11   10   09

To my past students, above all, Lisa

*If much in the world were mystery the limits of that world were not, for it was without measure or bound and there were contained within it creatures more horrible yet and men of other colors and beings which no man has looked upon and yet not alien none of it more than were their own hearts alien in them, whatever wilderness contained there and whatever beasts.*

CORMAC McCARTHY, *BLOOD MERIDIAN*

# CONTENTS

# ACKNOWLEDGMENTS

This book started out as a collaboration with my old friend since junior high school, Glenn Baaten. Having thought about and argued such things since our beginnings, it seemed appropriate to put something down on paper. Geography, lassitude on my part and the tyrannical drive of authorship soon got in the way of this joint project. What remains is my fault alone. Nevertheless, without Glenn's inspiration I would never have begun. Along the way I have also had much help with both my prose and the development of my ideas. Fritz Monsma early on put much time and effort into my clumsy prose and thinking. Later, Athan Aronis gave both encouragement and a critical reading essential to moving the work along. Finally Mike Foley and my editor, Gary Deddo, pushed me across the finish line with exactly the sort of correction and insight I needed. Above all, however, I must thank the many students I have taught at Boston College and St. Mary's College of California, who have given me the opportunity to work out the rhetorical presentation of the following material. I am not sure there is anything more exciting in life than talking about such things in the ever-changing and ever-new context of youthful human hearts, panting for something more and higher. To you, all my past students, I dedicate this book.

3 1833 05575 5638

# INTRODUCTION

*They won't let me. . . . I can't be . . . good!*

DOSTOEVSKY, *NOTES FROM UNDERGROUND*

The heart is deceitful above all things, and desperately wicked: who can know it?" (Jeremiah 17:9 KJV). With this claim of the prophet Jeremiah we begin. What are we to make of it? Could it be true about my heart? About your heart? Even if it were true, could we even know it? And if it is true, would we ever admit to it? More than likely our response to the claim is to recoil with indignation and anger. Who is Jeremiah to say such a thing! Not only is it not true, the very goodness we have within ourselves suggests that *he* is the wicked one, and that he speaks only of *his* heart! Perhaps. But then again, might not our indignation suggest that he is right? Quite often indignation is the best sign of a weak or even lost argument. Why are we so sure he is wrong? Do we really hunger and thirst for goodness so desperately that we cannot imagine wanting anything else? Is wickedness so awful that we cannot imagine being wicked or wanting to do wicked things for even one second? Or is it rather that we cannot imagine seeing ourselves as anything but good? All of us have a few failings here and there, no doubt; but *wicked?* Who could conceive of themselves in this way except the morbidly guilty, religious or paranoid?

Still, if our hearts *were* wicked, and, more importantly, deceitful—would this not be our very response? That is the question and the possibility we must pursue. Jeremiah is challenging us to an argument about who we are. Are we prepared to meet it head on, without distracting ourselves by turning angrily on the one who makes it? If we are, if we have even the minimal fortitude and focus to face this claim, how are we to find out if he is right? Further, if our hearts truly are this way, *should* we find it out, especially if we can't—or don't even want—to do anything about it? Yes, we should. For this simple reason: we—all of us—want to become good. Truly good. For this very best of reasons, if we remain deceived on this matter, the possible wickedness of our own heart, we will be deceived and unhappy in everything else.

In what follows—in the readings of ourselves, political philosophy, Greek tragedy and the Bible—and throughout all the twists and turns that may surprise us by their seeming perversity, we shall be in search of signs of the human heart: what it wants, what it fears and why it lies. Many strange topics—murder, incest and bloody scapegoating—will show up along the way. All these fugitive themes will turn out to be hidden paths to who we are. If we are to catch even a glimpse of our quarry, our own heart, we must not flinch, and we must have the courage to pursue the track wherever it leads.

Where it will lead is into a labyrinth. Like any labyrinth the way in is usually the way out—all we need is a thread. The thread we will follow is our desire. The desire to possess and the desire to be seen are what led us astray in the first place. To find our way back, we must pursue the desire to know, both ourselves and our true good. Unfortunately all three desires have become tangled up together in the knot we have made of ourselves.

To disentangle this knot, we must first perform an inward experiment whose results can only be verified in the mind and imagination of the reader. It is a simple experiment, imagining the powers of invisibility; but if it works, it will reveal what we would prefer to keep hidden within the privacy of our own body. If we can see what we want to keep private behind our bodily veil of skin, we can also see what we want to go public with in the political world of being seen before others.

To follow the thread of our political selves we must see how it is manifest in literature. Here, we not only turn inwards, but also outwards to see how we exist inside each other's heads. Politics will show us the human heart in the marketplace and in the theater of debate, interests, passions and rhetoric. But in the literary world of the ancient tragedians, we can see the intersection of the manifest and seen political world with the hidden and private world of life, death and sexuality.

If we follow the thread of our entangled desires to both hide and be seen, we will uncover many monsters. To slay them we must face them and see them for what they are. Above all, we must see that they are monsters of our own making. They are not other people. This is where the thread of our desire to know most often leads us astray. Instead of knowing ourselves, we want to know our enemies and those outside social pressures that keep us from releasing the goodness we imagine we harbor within. We turn without to seek, pursue and slay. For all the vaunted education and learning of our modern enlightened age, what it comes down to for us and our desire to be good is the cry of Dostoevsky's underground man: "*They* won't let me be good." Knowledge is a mere tool we must use to protect ourselves from others, even as we use it to get what we think we want from those same people. This is the monstrous deceit at the heart of who we are. To slay it we must know it. To know it is to find it not outside, but inside.

To know who we are, to get to the bottom of our labyrinthine heart and the wicked monsters hiding in all of us, we must truly want to know the truth. We must see for ourselves what we have made of ourselves, and confess the final and true confession of the underground man: "*I* can't be good." To do this we must reexamine two important traditions, classical political philosophy and the Bible. Both place the desire to know front and center, and yet both tell us mostly of our own deceit and wickedness. In both the Christian teaching on sin and the Greek demand to "know thyself," we find a tradition that does not flatter, does not compliment and takes very seriously the possibility that murder and mayhem are not far from any of us.

In what follows I will try to revive those traditions and the traditional way they get us to examine ourselves. In doing so, I know full well I will be going against the tide. But that is nothing new. Even in their own day, at the high tide of their persuasive reach, the teaching on sin or the demand for self-examination expected nothing but firm and tenacious resistance. If the heart was indeed desperate in its wickedness, then the deceit was above all things, then and now, in how we saw ourselves. Perhaps if we just go deep enough, keep our eye on the thread and stop looking around at others, we might someday slay our monsters and find our way back.

As we proceed keep in mind that each chapter is only a partial glimpse at who we are. Later chapters must build upon and bring out aspects of ourselves deliberately neglected in earlier chapters. There are reasons for this. The three desires that will guide us—the desire to have, the desire to be seen and the desire to know—roughly correspond to the three parts of the soul first elaborated in Plato's *Republic.* The question for Plato and ourselves, however, is not the identity of the parts but their ordering and relation to one another. Each part can be taken for the whole, and political philosophers that come along later will dwell more or less on one to the detriment of the other. Hobbes and Machiavelli, for example, have a lot to say about the desire to have and keep, but Rousseau sheds much more light on our desire to be seen. Only at the level of our desire to know do we attain a position to integrate the entire argument, and, possibly, ourselves. Plato and Aristotle together have come closest to doing this, and so not until the fifth chapter, "The Heart and Philosophy," will we get a full account of these parts all working together. Nevertheless, the burden of the book is to argue that even their account is not adequate to understand, much less properly order the desires that make us who we are.

For that we will need to look at the narrative of the Bible as it speaks to the mysteries of the human heart. The "heart" as used in the Bible is best understood in terms of Plato's middle part of the soul, what he calls *thumos.* As middle, that part must be understood in its relation both above and below, to *eros* and *logos.* For that reason one might read this entire work as an explication of thumos in both the Biblical and philosophical perspective. And it is that, at least. Even more, however, it is an argument that the God spoken of in the Bible alone can satisfy our heart's desire, and our heart's desire is to be good, truly good. Being good, it will turn out, requires of us an entirely new heart, born again out of the death of our old and wicked one. None of us can supply that requirement on our own. All we can do is see through enough of the deceit and wickedness of the old to cry out for something new. Who, if anyone, will hear that cry and respond is, when all is said and done, all that matters.

# 1

## THE RING OF TRUTH

*Some seek their good in authority, some in intellectual inquiry and knowledge, some in pleasure.*

*Others again, who have indeed come closer to it, have found it impossible that this universal good, desired by all men, should lie in any of the particular objects which can only be possessed by one individual and which, once shared, cause their possessors more grief over the part they lack than satisfaction over the part they enjoy as their own. They have realized that the true good must be such that it may be possessed by all men at once without diminution or envy, and that no one should be able to lose it against his will. Their reason is that this desire is natural to man, since all men inevitably feel it, and man cannot be without it, and they therefore conclude . . .*

PASCAL, *PENSÉES*

*There's the scarlet thread of murder running through the colourless skein of life, and our duty is to unravel it, and isolate it, and expose every inch of it.*

SHERLOCK HOLMES

Imagine that you have found a magical ring that allows you to disappear and appear whenever you like. Would you want to use it? Plato describes this as the ring of Gyges, a ring that allowed an obscure peasant to rise to the top of a kingdom after killing the king and stealing his wife. J. R. R. Tolkien, in more recent times, built his entire fantasy world around a Ring of Power that sets off a war to possess, use or destroy its power of invisibility. Such a ring would let you get what you want and control how you appear—in both the wanting and getting—to others. When you wear it your body disappears but your desires remain.

This combination is immensely appealing. What we want to find out is why. What is the connection between our body, our desires and our power to satisfy those desires? Already you have a ring of sorts because nobody can get inside your head and see what you are thinking. All of us can hide inside ourselves the desire for the things we want; but why should the power to hide on the outside be the key to getting them?

Put aside for the moment all the good you might do if you had this power of invisibility. Instead, pay attention to those few, or more likely, many, things you might want just for yourself. Here, this power over your visible body and actions would be especially sweet. Your private desires

---

Give each, the just man and the unjust, license to do whatever he wants, while we follow and watch where his desire will lead each. We would catch the just man red-handed going the same way as the unjust man out of a desire to get the better; this is what any nature naturally pursues as good, while it is law which by force perverts it to honor equality. The license of which I speak would best be realized if they should come into possession of the sort of power that it is said the ancestor of Gyges, the Lydian, once got. They say he was a shepherd toiling in the service of the man who was then ruling Lydia. There came to pass a great thunderstorm and an earthquake; the earth cracked and a chasm opened at the place where he was pasturing. He saw it, wondered at it, and went down. He saw, along with other quite wonderful things about which they tell tales, a hollow bronze horse. It had windows; peeping in, he saw there was a corpse inside that looked larger than human size. It had nothing on except a gold ring on its hand; he slipped it off and went out. When there was the usual gathering of the shepherds to make the monthly report to the king about the flocks, he too came, wearing the ring. Now, while he was sitting with the others, he chanced to turn the collet of the ring to himself, toward the inside of his hand; when he did this, he became invisible to those sitting by him, and they discussed him as though he were away. He wondered at this, and, fingering the ring again, he twisted the collet toward the outside, when he had twisted it, he became visible. Thinking this over, he tested whether the ring had this power, and that was exactly his result; when he turned the collet inward, he became invisible, when outward, visible. Aware of this, he immediately contrived to be one of the messengers to the king. When he arrived, he committed adultery with the king's wife and, along with her, set upon the king and killed him. And so he took over the rule.

*Plato* Republic *359c-360b*

---

would stay private, and yet you could move about in public with no one the wiser that you either had them or did what needed doing to satisfy them. At the same time, with the ring off and your body visible, you could do only what you wanted them to see so they would believe you are someone entirely different from who you are in private.

Given the effect of this ring, both on what you might do and how others view you, what does it tell us about who we are? Do we see ourselves differently? Probably not. For an obvious reason: how we see ourselves is how others see us—visible and manifest in our words and deeds, but not in our thoughts and desires. When we look at the proverbial "man in the mirror" we still only see how we look from the outside. We do not know ourselves from the inside out, but, as the image suggests, from the outside in. We see only what can be mirrored in the eyes of others—what they might see, and what they might approve of, or not, in that seeing. We "see ourselves" always as a body can be seen, always in the eyes of someone, perhaps even God, but "seen" nonetheless. If only we could hide that body and control that seeing.

This is the beauty of our experiment with an imaginary ring of power. The ring does not reveal or change how we "see" ourselves. Our "self-image," high or low, is not at stake here. Self-esteem will never equate to goodness unless we can learn to estimate in some other way than by seeing or being seen. What we need is knowledge. The experiment of the ring tries to make us own up to our hidden desires and hidden fears. We would do one thing with the ring on, another with it off. Why does being visible make such a difference? Who is this "self," changed so radically by being seen? Why are our desires so problematic? Why must so many of them be hid from others? We cannot simply want what we want. We desire,

---

Nietzsche describes the differing contrasts between "good and bad" and between "good and evil," in terms of what he calls "master morality" and "slave morality," respectively:

> In the first case, when the ruling group determines what is "good," the exalted proud states of the soul are experienced as conferring distinction and determining the order of rank. The noble human being separates from himself those in whom the opposite of such exalted, proud states finds expression: he despises them. It should be noted immediately that in this first type of morality the opposition of "good" and "bad" means approximately the same as "noble" and "contempt-ible." (The opposition of "good" and "evil" has a different origin.) One feels contempt for the cowardly, the anxious, the petty, those intent on narrow utility; also for the suspicious with their unfree glances, those who humble themselves, the doglike people who allow themselves to be maltreated, the begging flatterers, above all the liars: it is part of the funda-mental faith of all aristocrats that the common people lie. "We truthful ones"—thus the nobility of ancient Greece referred to

itself. . . . Slave morality is essentially a morality of utility.

Here is the place for the origin of that famous opposition of "good" and "evil": into evil one's feelings project power and dangerousness, a certain terribleness, subtlety, and strength that does not permit contempt to develop. According to slave morality, those who are "evil" thus inspire fear; according to master morality it is precisely those who are "good" that inspire, and wish to inspire, fear, while the "bad" are felt to be contemptible.

The opposition reaches its climax when, as a logical consequence of slave morality, a touch of disdain is associated also with the "good" of this morality—this may be slight and benevolent—because the good human being has to be *undangerous* in the slaves' way of thinking: he is good-natured, easy to deceive, a little stupid perhaps, *un bonhomie*. Wherever slave morality becomes preponderant, language tends to bring the words "good" and "stupid" closer together.

*Friedrich Nietzsche,* Beyond Good and Evil, *§260*

---

and right away we fear some sort of evil should we be seen and found out. Why, to put it harshly, are we such hypocrites, wanting to do what must be hid from others?

Perhaps we could investigate this more closely if we examined our use of the word *good*. The good, it would seem, is that which we desire, just as evil is that which we avoid. Yet if we put on our ring we just might find ourselves doing some things we consider evil and or no longer doing some things we consider good. What happened? Did we stop desiring the good when our visible body disappeared? Did we stop avoiding evil when we could avoid being seen? Or is there something about what we consider good and evil that is greatly affected by whether or not we can be seen? If so, perhaps we should rethink just what we mean by "good and evil."

Take another contrast, that between "good and bad." If we had complete power over our appearances, the good would indeed be what we seek just as the bad is what we avoid. *Bad* is the better word here to contrast with *good*, because what is bad never tempts us to do anything but the good. We are not tempted to step in dog dirt, which is why we would never call it evil. Instead, we call it "bad" with a spontaneous look of disgust. We need no arguments why we do not do things that are bad: they are simply *not* good, and good things, in this sense, need no argument because they are, simply, good—what else would one desire? "Good and bad" therefore correlate, as they should, with desire and avoidance. Nevertheless this correlation is seen most clearly only when we have complete power over how and when our body and its actions appear before others.

Take away that power and things change. In the situation most of us find ourselves in, what is "good" is not what we seek or even particularly want. What we actually want quite often turns out to be "evil." This is why what is evil tempts us through our desires away from what is "good." What, then, is this "good" from which evil tempts us away? It does not seem something we desire or seek directly, yet it remains something we find ourselves doing most of the time. Even though evil tempts us through our desires, we push against those desires as if our very life depended upon resisting them. We resist what we want, but the source of that resistance is not itself a "wanting." It feels more like an "avoiding," motivated by fear rather than desire. What are we so fearful of? Again the ring makes this obvious. We fear being seen doing or getting things in the eyes of other people.

When we contrast "good with evil," as we usually do, rather than contrasting "good with bad," what we implicitly reveal is our secret inner harmony with evil, coupled with an outer disharmony coming not from our desires but our fears—above all, our fear of being seen doing that evil by others.

This "good" is good for others, but not particularly good for me. What is "good," in contrast to what tempts us and what we call "evil," is what cuts off and stifles our inner desires. If we succumb to temptation and do what truly seems good to us, what we have done is bad to others. Why we don't succumb to temptation is not the desire for the good but rather the fear of the bad. We fear suffering things we spontaneously deem bad. We fear what people would think if they could see what we hide. We fear what would happen if those same hidden things were done by others. We fear losing the satisfaction of what we truly *do* desire. We fear no longer having the control and power to satisfy our future desires.

Fear does not seek, it avoids. Put together all our fears and they do not add up to one thing we want. Perhaps that is why what is "good" as opposed to evil loses interest for us the minute we are protected from our fears through various rings of power—be they wealth, celebrity or connections. Once we are safe, protected from our fears, the motivation to do "good" vanishes. It was only a shadow cast by our fear.

Take away our fears and we discover what we think our true good is, our true motivation, the wellspring of desire that does not change whether we have a ring on or not. It is the good revealed by our experiment. It is wickedness and evil. Or so we call it when we see it or suffer from it in others. Nevertheless it is our own secret and private good that makes us who we are; for it is the one good we can be sure we truly seek without the confusing double-talk of wanting to be seen as "good" in the eyes of someone else.

About the "good," then, we are gravely confused, not to mention downright deceitful. Especially when we look in the mirror and say "I am pretty good," or, at the very least, "not so bad." By this "good" we mean that we *appear* good to others, and we only bother to make this appearance in order to reduce their fear of us or our fear of them. Why, then, are we so proud of ourselves?

Being "good" in this sense is no more than being just in the lowest possible sense, the sense of merely obeying the law. This minimal demand may be for the best. Without it society would not function. Criminals won't play this game, and sociopaths can't. We try to force them into line with laws and punishments designed to give them more to be afraid of. The rest of us already are "good," apart from a few bad driving habits and questionable income tax forms. What else could it possibly mean, to be "good," if being good in this sense is already so easy?

Suppose that, ring or no ring, you would do the same things. The "invisible you" wants the same as the "visible you" professes to want. What you fear would be the same inside and out and would consist solely of *not* satisfying your desires. Your fears would only be your desires expressed negatively. Being visible would thus have no effect whatsoever on your ability to satisfy those desires. Evil would have no power to seduce you. It would be distasteful, no different from the bad. It couldn't tempt you, but could only keep you from what you really want—the good. Society may make laws and dole out bad reputations to make people afraid, but that is only training in pursuing a minimal good out of fear. You, instead, would need no law to pursue the good for you actually hunger and thirst for it. Now, and only now, would you *be* truly good. To be good takes the scare quotes off whatever good things or good actions you pursue, because, ring

---

But in the case of the virtues an act is not performed justly or with self-control if the act is itself of a certain kind, but only if in addition the agent has certain characteristics as he performs it: first of all, he must know what he is doing; secondly, he must choose to act the way he does, and he must choose it for its own sake; and in the third place, the act must spring from a firm and unchangeable character. . . . In other words, acts are called just and self-controlled when they are the kind of acts a just and self-controlled man would perform.

*Aristotle* Nicomachean Ethics *1105a30-1105b5, Ostwald translation*

---

or no ring, what you would do and what you would want stay the same. You would live in terms of the contrast between good and bad with no need to control your appearances to make it possible.

Are you truly good without scare quotes? Do you seek only what is good and avoid only what is bad? Do you want to *be* good and do you fear *not being* good more than you fear other people? The ring experiment should show you the truth. Few of us pass its test. All of us are deeply divided between our inner and outer selves. But let us be more forgiving, as we divide the sheep from the goats. Do you at least *want* to be good? If you do not hunger and thirst for goodness, do you at least wish you did?

Maybe not. After all, if the ring experiment reveals anything, it makes manifest what sort of "good" we really want, and it is certainly not being good as defined above. We do not usually want to *be* good, if that means to have within ourselves a good character, unchanging and stable, that wants on the inside the same deeds done on the outside.

Instead, what we want is to *have* what is good, and as the grammar suggests, to "have" what is good is to have good things. The good for us is always the good things that can be possessed, or, much worse, be lost. We want to possess the good, to keep what is good, and not lose it. Having is the wellspring of our desires. We do everything we do to get good things, things that are seen as good precisely because we want to have them and do not want to lose them.

Having good things is not just having stuff. We are not all shallow materialists. Even if we want such intangibles as fame, power or glory, all these are good *things* in the sense that they can be taken away from us to the same extent that they are given. The desire to be famous is the fear of also losing that fame. What the press giveth, the press taketh away, and who can control such a lord without an extreme servility? Even if we strive after the glory of a soldier or firefighter, such glory is bestowed or withheld by those who usually know nothing of what truly earns such glory. Opinions come and go, only the truth remains, even if no one knows it but yourself. Unfortunately, what most of us want are others' good opinions; few of us want to know if we truly *are* good.

Why so much hunger to *have* what is good, so little hunger to *be* good?

Of course, we say we want to be good. Most of us mean that we want to *have* the feelings that go along with being good. We want to have feelings of being good, and we don't want to lose those feelings. Take away those feelings (for they too are something we can have and so something that can be lost or taken) and we lose all interest in what may have initially caused them. When we talk about being good, our words point to a state, a settled character. But our real concern is with how we *feel* about ourselves, and this will show behind our words. We all want to "feel good about ourselves"; certain actions just don't "feel right"; we "feel guilty" if we do something wrong. If we could find a drug with no unpleasant side effects that would make us feel good about ourselves regardless of what we do or who we are, then we would take it, just as we would gladly put on the ring. How much of psychotherapy is the attempt to supply just such a drug without the chemistry?

I did not go into matters where, if I did go, I was going to be of no benefit either to you or to myself; instead, I went to each of you privately to perform the greatest benefaction, as *I* affirm, and I attempted to persuade each of you not to care for any of his own things until he cares for himself, how he will be the best and most prudent possible, nor to care for the things of the city until he cares for the city itself, and so to care for the other things in the same way.

*Plato* Apology of Socrates *36c*

The eclipse of the sense of God and of man inevitably leads to a practical materialism, which breeds individualism, utilitarianism and hedonism. Here too we see the permanent validity of the words of the Apostle: "And since they did not see fit to acknowledge God, God gave them up to a base mind and to improper conduct" (Rom. 1:28). The values of being are replaced by those of having. The only goal which counts is the pursuit of one's own material well-being. The so-called quality of life is interpreted primarily or exclusively as economic efficiency, inordinate consumerism, physical beauty and pleasure, to the neglect of the more profound dimensions— interpersonal, spiritual and religious—of existence. . . . Within this same cultural climate, the body is no longer perceived as a properly personal reality, a sign and place of relations with others, with God and with the world. It is reduced to pure materiality: it is simply a complex of organs, functions and energies to be used according to the sole criteria of pleasure and efficiency.

*John Paul II,* Evangelium Vitae, *§23*

Again, why are we like this? Why is being good of so little interest to us, and yet having good things, above all, good feelings, of maximal interest to us? The initial answer is that "who" we are more often than not relates to itself in terms of something we seem to have, the "what" of our own body. We relate to "who" we are in terms of "what" we have when we use our body as the first tool among many to get what we want, rather than an essential component of who we are. If we are "whos" who "have," all we know of ourselves is that having, and as much as that someone is distracted outwardly to what it has, it is fearful of what those other "whos" see and want in their own distraction. If our goodness were found in who we are, what we have or what others see would be of little concern. Unfortunately, the ring reveals how little concern we have in being who we are, and how much interest we have in having what we have. And above all, what we seem to have is our own body.

The source of the ring's power is that it makes what is usually visible before others, our body, invisible. Yet this same body is our first "possession" and locus of all further possessions. We want the sort of things a body can have, particularly in relation to other bodies, things that can be seen, touched, felt, heard, eaten and so forth. Nevertheless, the things a body can have can also be lost, withheld or taken by other bodies, bodies that also see, touch, feel, hear and eat. In the case of eating, what we eat—or, if you like, what we consume—cannot be eaten or consumed by anyone else. Insofar as we are consumers, then, what we "consume" relative to our bodies cannot be consumed by anyone else's body. Like a dog who wolfs down its food in a corner while keeping a sharp eye on every other dog, we too want to see everyone else's having even while keeping hidden our own.

Because of what we want—bodily things that one can possess or have—other "whos" who relate to their bodies in the same way stand in the way. To get what you want, and keep it, you need to control how those other bodies act, and more importantly, how those "whos" who have, think. How do we control what they think? By what they see of us and what they hear, and even more, by what they don't see and don't hear. In other words, we need our body both to show and to hide before others; but because our bodies can always be seen, we fall short of complete control. The ring could split our assets from our liabilities. An invisible body could get what we want without setting back the work of the visible body: showing itself to advantage. But our sight would be as keen and more so, to see the truth about others, behind their attempt to show themselves better than they are. Unfortunately everyone else is like us. We all try to make our bodies less vulnerable and the bodies of others more vulnerable—all because of our strange relation to our bodies in terms of both visibility and possession.

This is the world that the ring shows us. The ring shows what other bodies mean to us: we need them but fear them even more. They are obstacles and the source of all other obstacles. Everything we would want to

---

But the most frequent reason why men desire to hurt each other, ariseth hence, that many men at the same time have an appetite to the same thing; which yet very often they can neither enjoy in common, nor yet divide it; whence it follows that the strongest must have it, and who is strongest must be decided by the sword.

*Thomas Hobbes* De Cive *1.6*

---

possess, achieve or enjoy through the power of the ring we would want to enjoy as visible. But it is only as invisible that we could be sure of getting or keeping them.

In short, our problematic desires, but also our fears, arise from our possessive relation to our own body. The goods that we want are all goods that we could lose. Just as we all want the good opinion of others, if others see us in the wrong light, we lose that good opinion. Just as we want to be honored for deeds, if people see our other deeds we lose that honor. Just as we all want to be seen as unique and original, if people saw our slavish imitations and daily banality, we lose that reputation. Opinions, honor, reputation are all as much something we can possess as something we can lose. Possession in all its forms is our good, and our own body seems key to both why we want to possess and how we will gain and keep those possessions. To have any good thing we must possess life and possess our own body. But possessions, sadly, cannot be shared.

As with the proverbial cake, you can have it, *or* you can eat it. We can divvy out an equal piece of pie to all, but each piece goes to one body. Eat it and you can't eat it again. To have it again you will have to get another piece.

Relating to ourselves and our bodies in terms of possession transforms every good thing into that pie—all become ultimately unshareable. If our good is some sort of having, then we have to face down the problems and limitations of unshareability. Everything we have can also be lost or consumed. We must then find what we lost or get something new. Everything we have can be taken, and who will take them but that multitude of other humans who want to possess those very same things? Unshareability is *the* political problem, lurking behind all others; it is a life and death issue for all who would wear the ring.

Take the simplified example of a dinner party on stage or an enforced retreat of people trapped in a house for week. All, like ourselves, are tempted to wear the ring, which is to say, all find their visible bodies a

---

"Have we any greater evil for a city than what splits it and makes it many instead of one? Or a greater good than what binds it together and makes it one?"

"No we don't."

"Doesn't the community of pleasure and pain bind it together, when to the greatest extent possible all the citizens alike rejoice and are pained at the same comings into being and perishings?"

"That's entirely certain," he said.

"But the privacy of such things dissolves it, when some are overwhelmed and the others overjoyed by the same things happening in the city and those within the city?"

"Of course."

"Doesn't that sort of thing happen when they don't utter such phrases as 'my own' and 'not my own' at the same time in the city, and similarly with respect to 'somebody else's?"

"Entirely so."

"Is, then, that city in which most say 'my own' and 'not my own' about the same thing, and in the same way, the best governed city?"

"By far."

*Plato* Republic *462b-c*

---

threat to their own and each other's desires. What happens? Fears mount. Enjoyment shrinks. Tension is in the air as the sources of conflict multiply. Before long a body, unshareable source of all this desire for possession, makes a grand entrance. As a corpse. Which means there was a murder. Which means there must be a murderer.

All quite mysterious and dramatic! But it is only the drama and mystery the ring shows us. Just as the corpse—inert, blank possession, owning nothing, not even itself—is the epitome of all our fears, so too the murderer is the epitome of all our desires to get what we want and also get away with it. Our lust for the ring reveals us all as potential murderers. Deep down we may all suspect murder of our neighbors. But is that not because we all, with much better evidence, have reason to suspect ourselves? Why else are we so fascinated with murder mysteries? Everyone in the room, as we know from ourselves, might always have a motive. All our detective work presupposes self-knowledge, and yet we tend to concentrate on the other people in the room, for it is always someone other than the detective who has done the crime.

Where do these detectives get such intimate knowledge of the workings of the criminal mind? Is it because theirs is a specialized job, focusing on the worst elements of society? Or is it because they are human beings, after all, just like the rest of us? If our own detective work is working, we should now see ourselves as potential thieves, criminals and murderers. In addition, we should see we are all quite practiced and skillful liars because few of us are ever the "usual suspects."

If the possibility exposed by our ring experiment that we are all potential murderers and actual liars sounds a bit harsh and insulting, don't blame me or anyone else—blame yourself. Your secret lust for the ring is what stole your good reputation. All you can do to restore your honor is put a bit of self-knowledge where that reputation used to be. This knowledge requires no mirrors—no looking or being looked at—because it is an attempt to know yourself, free from appearances, before me or anyone else.

For the first time, you can truly wish you *were good,* or at least wish you did wish it, and *know what it is* you are desiring. If you do not know what you want, you can of course never get it. Waste your life wanting only good things that can be possessed, and you will blind yourself to the one good that cannot be lost. Even worse, you won't even get to keep the goods you think you want. Death will have the last word. As it draws nearer, it will bring fear with it, until it fills your whole life with fears. When life means having, death is the final defeat and failure, the loss of every good that the body can have. If we are ever to "keep" our good and not to lose it when we die, we must somehow seek what is good in an entirely different way.

In this first chapter we have merely done an experiment, and (I hope) opened our eyes to some home truths about ourselves that we are prone to overlook. The goal of this experiment, with its seemingly cynical and pessimistic accountings of ourselves, is not to lead us to despair. It is rather to elicit the desire to be truly good. Appearances won't do, even if they do "do" for each other and ourselves most of the time. We really

---

Well, what you call "the secret" is exactly the opposite. I don't try to get outside the man. I try to get inside the murderer. . . . Indeed it's much more than that, don't you see? I *am* inside a man, moving his arms and legs; but I wait till I know I am inside a murderer, thinking his thoughts, wrestling with his passions; till I have bent myself into the posture of his hunched and peering hatred; till I see the world with his bloodshot and squinting eyes, looking between the blinkers of his half-witted concentration; looking up the short and sharp perspective of a straight road to a pool of blood. Till I am really a murderer.

*G. K. Chesterton,* The Secret of Father Brown, *p. 13*

---

do want more than this. All of us have a still, small desire in ourselves to be good. It is as quiet and yet insistent as our desire to know. Before this overlooked desire can be fanned into flames, however, we must first know, in order to clear out, all the loud and clamoring fears and other desires that get in its way. The key to our heart's desire is knowing rather than having. And, initially at least, it is knowing just how desperately wicked our heart truly is.

# 2

## JUST FEARS

*It is hard to fight against anger [thumos] because what it wants to happen, it purchases in exchange for life.*

HERACLITUS FRAGMENT 85

So far we have dealt with our strange relation to our body that leads to an unshareable desire to have rather to be and with our lust for invisibility whereby our inside is not our outside. But our problem is not just that we relate to our body as private and unshareable, it is also that we live, each of us, in a "body politic." This body, the body of our lives together, raises the question of justice. Just as the body private raises questions about being good and having good things, the body politic raises questions about being just and appearing just. Every body politic will have some sort of constitution, which is to say, laws or customs to govern our interaction. The concrete question of justice asks whether we will comply with this constitution. When we get down to cases, the question is always whether we will obey a particular set of rules. We may recognize the authority of a law, God, a human being or a part of our own soul. But in each case justice will demand obedience, and our decision to obey or not to obey poses further questions about rule, such as, What motivates those who make the rules? Are the rules for my good or someone else's? The question of being good precedes the question of being just. How else could we say why we are, should be or refuse to be just, unless we can say what good we hope to achieve thereby?

To broach the question of justice, get into the heads of your neighbors. How would they deal with a lot of people just like you? All of them, you can count on it, are tempted just like you by the ring of power. How would a large gathering of such people live as a community? We all want what we could have, were we invisible. We fear what we might lose, being visible. How will this community arrange things, if each hopes to maximize our wants and minimize our fears?

The ring suggests a rude lesson about justice. If all of us secretly lust after invisibility, then we hold that injustice—doing what you want with

---

They say that doing injustice is naturally good, and suffering injustice bad, but that the bad in suffering injustice far exceeds the good in doing it; so that, when they do and taste of both, it seems profitable—to those who are not able to escape the one and choose the other—to set down a compact among themselves neither to do injustice nor to suffer it. And from there they began to set down their own laws and compacts and to name what the laws commands lawful and just. And this, then, is the genesis and being of justice; it is a mean between what is best—doing injustice without paying the penalty—and what is worst—suffering injustice without being able to avenge oneself. The just is in the middle between these two, cared for not because it is good but because it is honored due to a want of vigor in doing injustice.

*Plato* Republic 358e-359b

---

no regard to others—is naturally good. So confess our desires. But our fears reveal what we all deem as naturally bad—suffering injustice from our neighbors, especially when we suffer without taking revenge. What we naturally and spontaneously consider good and worth doing, we just as naturally and spontaneously consider bad if somebody does it to us. In short, being unjust seems good, but suffering injustice seems bad. Here lies the problem.

Surrounded by so many who desire to do so much injustice, the amount of injustice one can suffer is much greater than the injustice one can do. The fears of suffering injustices greatly outweigh the desire to do injustice. Shrewd and even not-so-shrewd calculators figure out that we need a common agreement to protect everyone from everyone else. If everyone would agree not to do what little injustices they might try on their own, fear would be massively reduced. This relief would be worth the small self-denial it would cost.

Everywhere there are public compacts that limit what we can do to others, and this would be the reasonable foundation of them. "Just" and "unjust" would be the names for what one can and cannot do. No one wants this justice for its own sake. It is a limit, a restriction, albeit one we need, because our fears exceed our desires. Obedience to the law is

---

Wherefore to seek peace, where there is any hopes of obtaining
it, and where there is none, to enquire out for auxiliaries of war,
is the dictate of right reason, that is, the law of nature.

*Thomas Hobbes* De Cive *1.15*

---

the only reasonable thing to do. As the contract becomes more comprehensive, bringing more and more subjects under its enforcement, it will be more "rational." The more rational, the more it will prove that crime does not pay. Only very bad calculators or those with no self-control will become criminals.

A case in point: our own constitution establishes "checks and balances." What needs to be checked but the intrinsic desire of all powers to overreach and get away with it? Yet every power fears overreaching from others. Balance is all. Yet we do not want balance for itself, but for the protection it gives.

What holds for governments holds even more for individuals. None of us want to be just—we do it out of fear. What are we afraid of? We are afraid of anyone not afraid, who will do what we truly want to do. Fear is good, even for oneself, since it makes us act "rationally," which is to say, safely and predictably to everyone else. Honesty, on the other hand, is bad. Honesty will make your particular desires stand out particularly. It will focus other's fears unfairly on you. This focused fear is as bad as the generalized fear is good. Pretense is reasonable where honesty is foolish. Pretend that the just actions forced on you by fear are your inner, natural and spontaneous desires. Pretend that the mask you put on out of fear is the real you. Act as though you do "just want to get along," without police, laws or punishment for motivation.

Do this well and you will start to believe it. You will become blind to your own hypocrisy, convinced that your inner desires match your outward actions. True believers never suspect that they are anything but entirely

---

In such a condition, there is no place for Industry; because the fruit thereof is uncertain; and consequently no Culture of the Earth; no Navigation, nor use of the commodities that may be imported by Sea; no commodious Building; no Instruments of moving, and removing such things as require much force; no Knowledge of the face of the Earth; no account of Time; no Arts; no Letters; no Society; and which is worst of all, continuall feare, and danger of violent death; And the life of man, solitary, poore, nasty, brutish, and short.

*Thomas Hobbes,* Leviathan, p. 186

---

just—inside and out—or that fear has anything to do with it. Let's face it, most of us are this way. That is why we need our ring. Getting close to the truth only makes us more fearful, giving pretense a greater hold on us. Only a strong device will show the truth to us.

Our economics will be like our justice, coming from fear and calculation.

This might seem odd. Here, if anywhere, we are free to pursue our desires. That's capitalism, right? But, again, not so fast. When capitalism works we can pursue, and we often get, what we desire. What becomes of our fears? Have they decreased? Not at all. Just the opposite. Everything we own increases our fear of loss. That's how possession, founded on the mortal body, works. As the saying goes, "the more possessions you own, the more they own you." To be "owned" by your possessions means your entire life is controlled and managed by your fear of losing them. The more you have, the more controlled and controllable you are.

Any political system that wants its citizens to behave should make them rich.

People who own things have to support the system in order to keep

---

The prince should nonetheless make himself feared in such a mode that if he does not acquire love, he escapes hatred, because being feared and not being hated can go together very well. This he will always do if he abstains from the property of his citizens and his subjects, and from their women; and if he also needs to proceed against someone's life, he must abstain from the property of others, because men forget the death of a father more quickly than the loss of a patrimony.

*Niccolo Machiavelli,* The Prince, *p. 67*

The passions that incline men to peace are fear of death, desire of such things as are necessary to commodious living, and a hope by their industry to attain them.

*Thomas Hobbes,* Leviathan, *p. 188*

Men at first, for the most part, contented themselves with what un-assisted nature offered to their necessities; and though afterwards, in some parts of the world, where the increase of people and stock, with the use of money, had made land scarce, and so of some value, the several communities settled the bounds of their distinct territories, and, by laws, within themselves, regulated the proper-ties of the private men of their society, and so, by compact and agreement, settled the property which labor and industry began.

*John Locke,* The Second Treatise on Government, *p. 45*

---

what they have. The poor have little to lose apart from their own body. That's why we give them so much to fear in the form of incarceration or physical punishment. But for keeping the peace, prisons and police are terribly inefficient. A nation that needs a cop on every corner is in trouble. Better the cop inside every head. Intrinsic coercion is the way to go, and what coerces the law-abiding are the internal fears that expand even as our possessions expand beyond the body. We don't realize it, but possession, fear and control go together. Sow desire and you reap servitude.

Of course we rarely notice this, and we are not meant to. We pursue what we think are our desires, getting things and the power to get more things. All this sweat and bustle hides our truly operating passion—the fear of loss and death. The desire for having increasingly becomes the fear of losing.

A junkie will lose the enjoyment of his drug, but stay dominated, in every waking moment, by the fear of suffering withdrawal if he loses that drug. Possession and having work in the same way. What would a junkie say is the dominating passion of his life? To get his fix. What is it that

---

I hope no body will doubt but that men would much more greedily be carried by nature, if all fear were removed, to obtain dominion, than to gain society. We must therefore resolve, that the original of all great and lasting societies consisted not in the mutual good will men had towards each other, but in the mutual fear they had of each other.

*Thomas Hobbes* De Cive *1.2*

---

truly dominates him? The fear of *not* getting his fix. Until the junkie admits this to himself, there is no cure. Our fear trumps our desire. We need to admit it, and to admit our need to hide that fear from others. This is hardly likely, since we hide it from ourselves. But we have no chance to be just or good until we do.

But we are getting ahead of ourselves. For all our talk of desire, we are leaving out an entire species of it, one that is at work wherever we are concerned with justice. To see this, let us turn directly to our "just" fears. What do we say when we suffer an injustice? "I want justice!" What do we want with this cry? Certainly it is no possession. We do not want ourselves to be just. We do not even want to undo the deed. It has already been done. What we want is revenge. What we fear is not getting revenge.

Suppose somebody steals your car and wrecks it. This is bad. You had a good thing, but now it is lost to you. Now suppose the thief is never

---

To which end we are to consider that the felicity of this life consists not in the repose of a mind satisfied. For there is no such *finis ultimus,* utmost aim, nor *summum bonum,* greatest good, as is spoken of in the books of the old moral philosophers. Nor can a man any more live whose desires are at an end than he whose senses and imagination are at a stand. Felicity is a continual progress of the desire from one object to another, the attaining of the former being still but the way to the latter. The cause whereof is that the object of man's desire is not to enjoy once only and for one instant of time, but to assure forever the way of his future desire.

*Thomas Hobbes,* Leviathan, *pp. 160-61*

---

caught and punished. This is even worse. First no car, and now no justice. Having no car depressed you. Having no justice enrages you. But wait. What is this extra loss, after the car was already entirely gone? The desire for justice must be different from the desire for having something good. Somehow you have found an extra wrong that is getting you all worked up. Why the rage?

The rage comes from a largely ignored part of the soul. The Greeks had a word for it. The *thumos* is your chest or "heart," and so rage is the *thumotic* passion. This part of the soul rages when you are enraged. When passion inflames a crowd, it catches fire.

Road rage is thumotic passion. "I need to move, but he is in my way" is merely a common frustration in traffic. "I, representing sensible people, will punish him for violating universally recognized rules of proper driving!" is indignant, thumotic road rage. Grasp the difference and you recognize thumotic passion, and you have an inkling of the natural connection between justice and rage.

Thumos is a strangely contagious passion. This is why we associate it with crowds. It unites you with your comrade against a common enemy. It grows in imitative response to someone else's indignation towards you. Why are there riots at soccer games in England? How does a fight at a baseball game become a brawl so quickly? "A bench-clearing brawl" say the sportswriters, and the oddity—no one was left behind on the bench, and the whole team became angry in the same instant—fails to strike us. Violent, indignant madness can change a peaceful game into a battle in a single moment. Which of us, alone, would say "Crucify him" and "give us Barabbas"? Why is it not surprising that a crowd could do so?

---

"This speech," I said, "certainly indicates that anger sometimes makes war against the desires as one thing against something else. . . ."

"And what about when a man supposes he's doing an injustice?" I said. "The nobler he is, won't he be less capable of anger at suffering hunger, cold or anything else of the sort inflicted on him by one whom he supposes does so justly; and, as I say, won't his spirit [thumos] be unwilling to rouse itself against this man?"

"True," he said.

"And what about when a man believes he's being done an injustice? Doesn't his spirit in this case boil and become harsh and form an alliance for battle with what seems just; and, even if it suffers in hunger, cold and everything of the sort, doesn't it stand firm and conquer, and not cease from its noble efforts before it has succeeded, or death intervenes, or before it becomes gentle, having been called in by the speech within like a dog by a herdsman?"

*Plato* Republic *440b-d*

---

Let us look more closely at this passion. We all experience it, but we don't think those experiences through. Take again the case of road rage. A man weaves through traffic, swerving in and out of crowded lanes at high speeds, forcing other drivers to slam on their brakes. Say you see all this in your rearview mirror. The car approaches and gets behind you, and is walled in by a large truck in the other lane. You slow down. The driver honks, flashes his brights. You go even slower. "That will teach him," you say to yourself.

What are you doing? What exactly are you "teaching," and who gave you the authority? Who are you to this stranger anyway—you are acting like his mother! Now the car honks, it begins to tailgate and threatens to hit your bumper. The driver now seems to be outraged by you. The nerve! You are not afraid. In fact, you are now hopping mad! Can you feel the thumos rising in your chest? You tap your brakes, you warn him. He doesn't slow down. You now contemplate slamming on your brakes, knowing full well this may cause an accident that may injure someone—possibly even yourself. But still, you don't care. By this time you have your back up, and your educational project has turned into open conflict in which you are willing to kill your erstwhile student and possibly even get killed yourself in the process. Behold thumos.

What starts as a seeming disinterested desire to teach justice flares up into a murderous passion that is just as willing to kill as be killed. This is the passion of the soldier, the policeman and the warrior—and of the lynch mob. Suffer injustice and this passion will torment you, goading you to take vengeance. Go to an action movie and you will feel the thumotic passion of the crowd. The audience will rise as one when Rambo (or The Rock, or whoever Hollywood will give us next) blows the villain away. Ever wonder why these movies are thrilling in a packed theater, but mildly boring if you have to watch them alone? Thumos is a group thing.

What does this passion want? Nothing. Literally no thing. It does not want to have or consume. Loss it does not fear because it doesn't want to possess, as simple desires do. This passion desires a notion, an idea. It wants a state of affairs. The world is out of joint and thumos wants to put it right. It wants, in a word, justice.

Thumos does not want to know about justice. To examine cases, to deliberate over what is right—thumos can't distinguish this from waver-ing. Wavering means weakness, and thumos will be strong, standing tall on the justice it affirms. It wants to salute justice, and then teach, witness, fight, kill or be killed, in service to that justice.

Our simple desires want to possess. They are self-interested. Thumos is willing to die for a notion. It will risk the foundation of all having, the living body, for a principle. Yet it is not entirely disinterested. It does want

---

Each one began to look at the others and to want to be looked at himself, and public esteem had a value. The one who sang or danced best, the handsomest, the strongest, the most adroit or the most eloquent became the most highly regarded. . . . From these first preferences were born vanity and contempt, on the one hand, and shame and envy on the other. . . . As soon as men had begun mutually to value one another, and the idea of esteem was formed in their minds, each one claimed to have a right to it, and it was no longer possible for anyone to be lacking it with impunity.

*Jean-Jacques Rousseau,* Discourse on the Origins of Inequality, *p. 64*

I would note how much that universal desire for reputation, honors, and preferences, which devours us all, trains and compares our talents and strengths; how much it excites and multiplies the pas-sions; and, by making all men competitors, rivals, or rather enemies, how many setbacks, successes and catastrophes of every sort it causes every day, by making so many contenders run the same course. I would show that it is to this ardor for making oneself the topic of conversation, to this fervor to distinguish oneself which nearly always keeps us outside ourselves, that we owe what is best and worst among men, our virtues and vices, our sciences and our errors, our conquerors and our philosophers, that is to say, a multitude of bad things against a small number of good ones.

*Jean-Jacques Rousseau,* Discourse on the Origins of Inequality, *p. 78*

---

something in return for its service to justice, but it is not property. What it wants is glory, a pat on the head, approval in someone's real or imagined eyes that one is worthy of honor or esteem.

Thumos is that in us which loves justice, glory, honor, victory and rank—and which can also drive us completely mad. It is the source all our glory and all our shame. It is what we fear in murderous gangland thugs, and it is what we praise in our brave soldiers. Each serves a justice radically different from the other, but both will die for honor and respect.

Thumos wants what *ought* to be. But how strange. Our appetite to possess things leads to the various laws designed to control others through fear. We make justice out of this low material by calculation and a paltry rationality, in order to keep others from our things and our persons. This is no way to breed respect for others or for ourselves. But the appetite for the "ought," for the justice that thumos seeks, loves and defends, is an appetite or passion that commands our loyalty and self-respect. It is an appetite for justice that calls us out of ourselves to serve something higher. It ennobles us because it is in the imagined eyes of that justice that we admire ourselves, or contrarily, feel ashamed. Like a dog wagging its tail at its master, we live for its praise and ranking even more than we live for our supply of treats or comforts.

Thumos does not free us from our lust for the power of the ring. The power of invisibility is, if anything, even more pronounced when it comes to this crucial aspect of who we are. As much as we may want to please and are ennobled by living up to our notion of justice, we are also dismissive, derisive and downright lethal to others who do not live up to it. To attain the former we must be seen. To avoid suffering the latter we must hide.

Desire, or *eros* (to use the Greek term contrasted with *thumos*) wants to acquire, possess and keep. It wants to skulk and thieve. Hence its lust for the ring. Thumos wants to show. It tempts us to reveal ourselves, to glory in being seen—in the best light, of course. To reveal ourselves to advantage, there is a great deal others must not see. To shine we hide our dross, the fear of death and all the lesser fears that follow inevitably on desire. As many things as there are to show with pride, there are perhaps more things of which we are ashamed—so we must somehow cover ourselves and hide. If we are nonetheless found out, or think we will be, we blush.

Don't you know that the beginning is the most important part of every work and that this is especially so with anything young and tender? For at that stage it's most plastic, and each thing assimilates itself to the model whose stamp anyone wishes to give it.

*Plato* Republic 377b

In other words, acts are called just and self-controlled when they are the kind of acts a just and self-controlled man would perform; but the just and self-controlled man is not he who performs these acts, but he who performs them in the way just and self-controlled men do.

*Aristotle* Nicomachean Ethics *1105b5-9, Ostwald translation*

We may thus conclude that virtue or excellence is a characteristic involving choice, and that it consists in observing the mean relative to us, a mean which is defined by a rational principle, such as a man of practical wisdom would use to determine it.

*Aristotle* Nicomachean Ethics *1106b36-1107a3, Ostwald translation*

It is reasonable to say that the poetic art as a whole was brought into being by two kinds of causes, both of them natural: for (1) imitating is innate in men from childhood, and it is in this respect that men differ from the other animals, namely, that they are the most imitative of animals and learn first by imitating, and (2) all men enjoy works of imitation.

*Aristotle* Poetics *1448b3-9, Apostle translation*

Think of it: the blush. It is the signature of thumos, just as it is the signature of our difference from all other animals. As Mark Twain once said, "Man is the only animal that blushes, or needs to." When we blush we reveal on the surface of our bodies that there is nothing truly private about us at all, that we have an inner and outer self, and that what is right, proper, just, chaste and so on, makes us somehow who we are in relation to other human beings. We are never truly alone in our inner self, for it can always make a social appearance in a blush. Likewise, if we have ever blushed for shame by ourselves, we can see that even in our own private imaginations we live in a social and political world that must somehow always make an appearance before others.

The blush *and* the flush of thumotic anger reveal a depth to our desire for invisibility that goes far beyond the body. We are not just bodies, as we are not just animals. We are the animal that must learn almost everything through imitation, especially what we want. Food, water, shelter—

---

By "self-sufficient" we do not mean an individual who leads just a solitary life, but one with parents and children and a wife and, in general, with friends and fellow-citizens as well, since man is by nature political.

*Aristotle* Nicomachean Ethics *1097b8-10, Apostle translation*

[M]an is by nature a political animal. He who is without a city through nature rather than chance is either mean or superior to man; he is "without clan, without law, without hearth," like the person reproved by Homer; for the one who is such by nature has by this fact a desire for war, as if he were an isolated piece in a game of chess.

*Aristotle* Politics *1253a1-10*

---

we have few true needs. The bulk of our desires grow in us as we watch others and imitate their desires.

Whom then do we imitate? Those who are above us in rank or social status, beginning with daddy and mommy. We want to be just like our parents, so we want to have what they deem worth having. When we get older, we figure out that their desires also came through the imitation of others, and so we start imitating those whom our parents imitate. This system of rank in our imitating keeps going up until we get to some sort of God or godlike celebrity who, as the richest, most prestigious or most famous, tells everyone below what they must aspire to in their imitative desire.

---

The principal source of violence between human beings is mimetic rivalry, the rivalry resulting from imitation of a model who becomes a rival or of a rival who becomes a model. Such conflicts are not accidental, but neither are they the fruit of an instinct of aggression or an aggressive drive. Mimetic rivalries can become so intense that the rivals denigrate each other, steal the other's possessions, seduce the other's spouse, and finally, they even go so far as murder. . . . the four major acts of violence prohibited by the four commandments that precede the tenth.

*René Girard,* I See Satan Fall Like Lightning, *p. 11*

Since the objects we should not desire and nevertheless do desire always belong to the neighbor, it is clearly the neighbor who renders them desirable. In the formulation of the prohibition, the neighbor must take the place of the objects, and indeed he does take their place in the last phrase of the sentence that prohibits no longer objects enumerated one by one but "anything that belongs to him [the neighbor]." What the tenth commandment sketches, without defining it explicitly, is a fundamental revolution in the understanding of desire. We assume that desire is objective or subjective, but in reality it rests on a third party who gives value to the objects. The third party is usually the one who is closest, the neighbor. To maintain peace between human beings, it is essential to define prohibitions in light of this extremely significant fact: our neighbor is the model for our desires. This is what I call mimetic desire.

*René Girard,* I See Satan Fall Like Lightning, *pp. 9-10*

---

Here, then, we see why the "pink-cheeked animal" who blushes is also the "political animal."

We are so thoroughly saturated with imitation that we have no desires that are not common, no matter how inwardly we feel them, no matter how private they seem to us. The hive of us, stratified by a standard of rank peculiar to ourselves, continually gaze up with envy and glance down with apprehension. Together we make common objects of public desire that no outsider would possibly want. Our need to hide does not come from an intimate or bodily aloneness. On the contrary, it comes from the presence in us of a teeming and roiling social drama that is quite literally scandalous. What we trip over in each other is that each of us stand in the way of getting what each of us show us we should want.

The Greek word *skandalon* means obstacle or (in the phrase familiar from the Gospels) stumbling block. Imitation is scandalous: it multiplies obsta-

---

O generations of men, how I
count you as equal with those who live
not at all!
What man, what man on earth wins more
of happiness than a seeming
and after that turning away?
Oedipus, you are my pattern of this,
Oedipus, you and your fate!

*Sophocles* Oedipus the King *1189-1196*

---

cles. When we want a thing the odds are that we want it through imitation. We only mimic the desire of another. If someone we deem slightly above us has or wants something, we want the same thing. Yet because our model already wants or has the thing, he becomes a *skandalon*, an obstacle in the way of my getting it. If I admire a man I will imitate him. He will have what I want by definition. His having it is why I want it. Having what I want, he becomes my rival. Now I hate him, because I admired him. He is the stumbling block between me and what I desire. I want to fight him, to clear the way to what he taught me to want. As my model, he inspired my erotic desire to possess and my thumotic desire to please. As my rival, he generates my erotic fear of loss and my thumotic passion to fight.

Consider the oddity of our human situation. As the animal with a minimum of instinctive desires, the bulk of our education consists of training us into and away from desires none of us have to begin with. As our parents try to raise us properly, modeling and rivalry, operating at cross purposes, shape us in their own way. How do we ever get beyond even our initial situation, wherein daddy implicitly tells us what we should want—mommy—even while he stands in the way, so to speak, of us ever getting her? Should we kill him and sleep with her? We blush for shame at the very thought, which may well mean we have somehow had that thought. But who outside of Oedipus in the story has ever done such a thing?

Nobody. How, then, did we all survive the potential rivalry of our models, beginning with our parents? Through deceit. By hiding. By somehow covering ourselves. By ordering our inside hearts and outside bodies in such a way that we show only our modeling and desire to please those

---

This shows that, if babies are innocent, it is not for lack of will to do harm, but for lack of strength. I have myself seen jealousy in a baby and know what it means. He was not old enough to talk, but whenever he saw his foster-brother at the breast, he would grow pale with envy. Mothers and nurses say that they can work such things out of the system by one means or another, but surely it cannot be called innocence, when the milk flows in such abundance from its source, to object to a rival desperately in need and depending for his life on the one form of nourishment? Such faults are not small or unimportant, but we are tender-hearted and bear with them because we know the child will grow out of them. It is clear that they are not mere peccadilloes, because the same faults are intolerable in older persons.

*Augustine* Confessions *1.7*

---

above us, even as we hide our rivalry and jealousy. The price is that our jealousy smolders inside us and threatens to explode.

All of this is quite apparent in children. If we step outside of our romantic yearning for an idyllic and innocent youth and look at what truly is, we will see that children are titanic in their thumotic rivalries, competitions and lusts for possession. If babies had the strength and status of adults they would tear society apart. Happily for them and us they are small.

Before they grow big they learn that rank is irreproachable. A child learns due regard for adults and other figures of authority, or authority

---

"Because it will be a necessity for them to use many drugs," I said. "Presumably we believe that for bodies not needing drugs, but willing to respond to a prescribed course of life, even a common doctor will do. But, of course, when there is also need to use drugs, we know there is need of the most courageous doctor."

"True, but to what purpose do you say this?"

"To this," I said. "It's likely that our rulers will have to use a throng of lies and deceptions for the benefit of the ruled. And, of course, we said that everything of this sort is useful as a form of remedy."

*Plato* Republic *459c-d*

ATHENA:

                              You have your power,
        you are goddesses—but not to turn
        on the world of men and ravage it past cure.
        I put my trust in Zeus and . . . must I add this?
        I am the only god who knows the keys
        to the armoury where his lightening-bolt is sealed.
        No need of that, not here.

                              Let me persuade you.

*Aeschylus* The Eumenides *833-840, Fagles translation*

So a prudent orderer of a republic, who has the intent to wish to help not himself but the common good, not for his own succession but for the common fatherland, should contrive to have authority alone; nor will a wise understanding ever reprove anyone for any extraordinary action that he use to order a kingdom or constitute a republic. It is very suitable that when the deed accuses him, the effect excuses him; and when the effect is good, as was that of Romulus, it will always excuse the deed; for he who is violent to spoil, not he who is violent to mend, should be reproved.

*Niccolo Machiavelli,* Discourses of Livy, *p. 29*

The specific political distinction to which political actions and motives can be reduced is that between friend and enemy. . . . The enemy is not merely any competitor or just any partner of a conflict in general. He is also not the private adversary whom one hates. An enemy exists only when, at least potentially, one fighting collectivity of people confronts a similar collectivity. The enemy is solely the public enemy, because everything that has a relationship to such a collectivity of men, particularly to a whole nation, becomes public by virtue of such a relationship.

*Carl Schmitt,* The Concept of the Political, *pp. 26-28*

---

will teach him to regret his ignorance. This will check his rivalry while encouraging his imitative modeling.

So long as rank is maintained thumos will be satisfied. Rank allows us to embrace the model of our desires while forswearing their possession or satisfaction apart from those who gave them to us. Thumos wants justice and is satisfied by vertical (that is, ranked high in contrast to low) authority, because its desire is more aware of its origin in persons rather than in things. Maintain that rank and ordering, and all will be well. But sooner or later rank will break down. As we grow up, models come down to our own level, and the desires modeled by others collide with the horizontal rivalries also presented. Soon a contagious violence erupts. Brothers fight with brothers fighting for and against the very same things in themselves.

From this rivalry comes, inevitably, a murder: a murder with immense political and religious significance. Cain, founder of the first city, killed his brother Abel. Romulus, founder of Rome, killed his brother Remus. The founding of every great political order is preceded by fratricide. Before there could be an American Republic there had to be a war between rival groups of the King's subjects. Society hides and represses rivalry, and yet is always careful to remember these original murders. Histories are written to preserve them. Myths are woven out of them. Rituals are built around them. Almost all religions celebrate sacrifices and shed real or symbolic blood.

Politics demands loyalties that are thicker than water. We must be willing to die for our fellow citizens, just as we are willing to kill foreigners. This murder will create for us a political division between modeling and rivalry that will allow us to live with our fellow citizens as friends only at the expense of someone else as enemies. To accomplish this, however, we must lie to ourselves. A murder and a lie. That is what we share in, what is communal, in our community of so-called justice.

# 3

## EROTIC AND
## THUMOTIC DESIRE

*For this consciousness has been fearful, not of this or that particular thing or just at odd moments, but its whole being has been seized with dread; for it has experienced the fear of death, the absolute Lord. . . . [A]lthough the fear of this lord is indeed the beginning of wisdom, consciousness is not therein aware that it is a being-for-self. Through work, however, the bondsman becomes conscious of what he truly is.*

G. W. F. HEGEL, *PHENOMENOLOGY OF SPIRIT*

Like a magician, it might seem, I have twice pulled the rabbit of murder out of the hat in the last chapters. Yet I am no magician. The rabbit of wicked murder was there all along, hidden by our own collective and individual self-deceit. Murder always surprises us, catches us off guard, but our hearts are nevertheless quietly brooding upon it continually in both our fears and desires. Perhaps if we slow down and watch the movements of our own hearts more deliberately, we can see how this not so cuddly beast got there in the first place.

The desire to have or possess, with all its bodily, sexual and economic ramifications, we have called *eros*. Eros is that appetite in us to have and keep those bodily things that of their very nature cannot be shared. What I have, you cannot share; and what you have, I cannot share. In times of abundance this is not so much a problem, but in times of scarcity this unshareability of erotic desire can be dangerous. The real problem, however, comes in with thumos.

If our erotic desires were the limited necessary desires we share with animals, there would be little competition and Mother Nature's generosity would probably be enough. What troubles us is that our merely animal

---

"So that we don't discuss in the dark," I said, "do you want us to define the necessary and the unnecessary desires?"

"Yes," he said, "that's what I want."

"Wouldn't those we aren't able to turn aside justly be called necessary, as well as all those whose satisfaction benefits us? We are by nature compelled to long for both of these, aren't we?"

"Quite so."

"Then we shall justly apply the term necessary to them."

"That is just."

"And what about this? If we were to affirm that all those are unnecessary of which a man could rid himself if he were to practice from youth on and whose presence, moreover, does no good—and sometimes even does the opposite of good—would what we say be fine?"

"Fine it would be."

*Plato* Republic *558d-559a*

---

appetites rarely set for us a limit to our desires. Instead, thumos, our desire to be seen, our appetite for honor and praise from others, leads us to imitate other people, and we imitate above all else by finding erotically desirable what they find desirable. Eros is infected through and through by our thumotic imagination and consequently almost all our desires become for us unnecessary.

Desire is now no longer tethered to the body; it is given free rein to expand through the imagination. An expanding erotic desire now makes nature seem more and more stingy, and our slices from its unshareable pie become smaller and smaller. At the same time, our thumotic nature leads us to models, those persons who in setting for us a desire for this pie, are precisely the ones most likely to stand in the way of our getting it or eating it. This unshareability is not just a quantitative increase in our fear of not being satisfied, it is even more so a qualitative increase in our anger at not getting what we want when we think we *ought* to get it. We have now forgotten the pie entirely and want something else—justice—manifest in our angry desire for vengeance.

If our rival gets the pie, it is not just bad; it is unfair. Our rival no longer shares in our ordered world of what ought to be, he has now stepped

---

For presumably, Adeimantus, a man who has his understanding truly turned towards the things that *are* has no leisure to look down toward the affairs of human beings and to be filled with envy and ill will as a result of fighting with them. But, rather, because he sees and contemplates things that are set in regular arrangement and are always in the same condition—things that neither do injustice to one another nor suffer it at one another's hands, but remain all in order according to reason—he imitates them and, as much as possible, makes himself like them. Or do you suppose there is any way of keeping someone from imitating that which he admires and therefore keeps company with?

*Plato* Republic 500c

---

radically outside into the angering world of rivalry and potentially violent competition over increasingly unshareable possessions. The unshareability built into us at the level of the body has now increased sevenfold into the thumotic unshareability of the heart. This unshareability threatens to grow like a cancer. All of our erstwhile models who shared with us in our thumotic world of the "good," "just" and "fair," if they stand in our way when we encounter the unshareability of bodies and things in nature, can quickly become monstrous rivals of raw "injustice." The only cure for this shift is rank; if their modeling is so unapproachably above us they can never stand in our way as rivals.

As long as sons honor and defer to fathers, privates respect and obey generals, and youth in general respects old age and tradition, our days shall be long in the land. We can give up our share of possession for a share in the honor we give them and they give us through our admiration and obedience to their higher political world of justice.

Nevertheless, as much as our thumotic nature wants and needs true justice, order and rank, the problem is that thumos has no idea what jus-

---

The beggar picked by Apollonius recalls the kind of homeless persons whom Athens and the great Greek cities fed at their expense in order to make use of them as *pharmakoi* when the appointed time arrived, that is, collectively to assassinate them—why back away from the proper term?—during the Thargelia and other Dionysian festivals. . . . The beggar stoned displays all the classical features of the *pharmakos,* features we see likewise in all the human victims of sacrificial rituals. To avoid arousing reprisals, the torturers choose social nobodies: the homeless, those without family, the disabled and ill, abandoned old people, all those in short who bear the preferential signs for being selected as victims. . . . These signs or features change hardly at all from one culture to another. Their constancy contradicts cultural relativism.

*René Girard,* I See Satan Fall Like Lightning, *pp. 76-77*

---

tice is or what a genuine standard of rank would be. Like a dog who has no choice in its master even while doomed to follow him loyally, thumos must take as just whatever is given to it. The desire to be seen and approved of in somebody's eyes is not the same as the desire to know what that approval is worth. So thumos must be given something. But if no one knows what justice truly is, then it must take something, and what it takes for itself is some sort of victim, a scapegoat.

In Greek, a scapegoat is called a *pharmakos* because it is functionally related to a *pharmakon,* or drug (as in our *pharmacy*). Like all drugs it is equal parts poison and cure.

The scapegoat cures the inevitable collapse of our models into rivals—inevitable because we cannot thumotically ground our justice or rank in knowledge. When our modeling fathers turn into our rivalrous brothers, all hell breaks loose and we become surrounded on all sides by enemies who would do us in, even as they think the same as us. This murderous social plague of all against all, if it cannot be stopped, would destroy everything and everyone. The stop is the scapegoat. A scapegoat (arbitrarily chosen, because everyone in this plague is equally an enemy of everyone else) gets singled out as the source of everyone else's fear and anger. The victim is thus the final target of the contagious thumotic anger of crowds, who in being singled out as guilty of the unending injustice in a crowd of rivals, can now focus that anger and purge it by remaking as innocent everyone but the victim. When the scapegoat is dead, justice suddenly seems satisfied. The lynched victim, the strange fruit of our collective fears and desires, hangs above everyone on a tree. The vertical ordering of justice is now shockingly manifest. Astonished by our own savagery, we are suddenly calm.

With that calm we seem to have solved our problem. If this murder has cured our injustice, then it must have been a just murder. The scapegoat was surely the poison among us, or how did his death cure us? In the

---

"So the real lie is hated not only by the gods, but also by human beings."

"Yes, in my opinion."

"Now what about the one in speeches? When and for whom is it also useful, so as not to deserve hatred? Isn't it useful against enemies, and, as a preventative, like a drug *[pharmakon]*, for so called friends when from madness or some folly they attempt to do something bad? And, in the telling of the tales we were just now speaking about—those told because we don't know where the truth about ancient things lies—likening the lie to the truth as best we can, don't we also make it useful?"

*Plato* Republic *382c-d*

---

victim's death and its aftermath, the poisonous nature of his guilt is proved by the restorative powers of his death. The plague of thumotic scarcity has ceased for a time, and a new order of justice can now give us back our rank and peaceable imitation.

Of course it is all a lie, a trick. It is self-deception of the highest order, but it works. In fact, it works so well that some sort of victim of murder can be found at the heart of all political and religious notions of justice. The thumotic madness of hearts evidenced in even the simplest case of road rage is the political problem par excellence, and the solution to that political problem has always involved some sort of bloodshed. If brother cannot live with brother, then there can be no city and hence no politics. If one brother can be singled out as no longer a brother but an enemy, then for the first time the other brothers can be friends. Within a family this problem can be mitigated as long as there remains an irreproachable father. But for brothers who must themselves grow up into fathers the vertical effect of patriarchy must be replaced with the horizontal effect of enemies as scapegoats. Why this should be true is a mystery, but it is the mystery at the heart of politics, which is to say, our very own heart. Who, indeed, can know it?

Even if we can only know the latent murderousness of our political relations by looking at our sacred tales of foundings in terms of bloodshed, such a glimpse is only out of the corner of our eye, since the sleight of hand built into them works through that very distraction. We see and yet we don't see. Whatever corpses there are lie safely half-buried in the past. What we can see more clearly is that most of us have little respect for ourselves. Consider the standard and widespread contempt for the bourgeoisie. Who are these contemptible folk but city-dwelling, middle-class people just like ourselves? Yet the reason *bourgeois* is such a term of reproach, particularly on the Left and in Europe, is because it manifests exactly who we are in the comfortable guise of somebody else. Consider the usual reproach against the bourgeois, "When it comes to what they want, they think only of themselves, when it comes to who they are, they think only of others." The two halves of this definition nicely mirror the problem of our erotic and thumotic desire.

The ring of power reveals the truth of the first half. When it comes to wanting we think only of ourselves, even if our fears cause us to apparently think of others. Discovering this in others we grow indignant at their selfishness, but our own putative "unselfishness" is merely the result of a more thoroughgoing triumph of our fears over our desires. Other's fears make them more agreeable to us, and our own fears make us more agreeable to them. Behind all that fear is the erotic desire that thinks only of itself and how it can either get or keep whatever it can for itself alone. Force and the threat of force are thus the glue of community because all of us are thinking only of ourselves when we deal with others. What we want for ourselves because of other selves is safety, safety both from one another and from our fears in general.

None of this, in ourselves or in others, is a pretty sight. Yet because we are thumotic as well as erotic, what we want to see in ourselves—even if not so much in others—is something beautiful and worth looking at. So

---

And because he knew that past rigors had generated some hatred for Remirro, to purge the spirits of that people and to gain them entirely to himself, he wished to show that if any cruelty had been committed, this had not come from him but from the harsh nature of his minister. And having seized this opportunity, he had him placed one morning in the piazza at Cesena in two pieces, with a piece of wood and bloody knife beside him. The ferocity of this spectacle left the people at once satisfied and stupefied.

*Niccolo Machiavelli,* The Prince, *p. 30*

---

we look at each other looking at us, and what we are looking for is meaning, particularly the meaning of *who* we are in the eyes of others. Safety and security from our fears is not nearly enough when it comes to this looking for who we are. Our desire for recognition trumps even our desire for possessions. All our getting or losing must mean something, and who can confer that meaning but the very people we want to take from or who might take from us?

We need to look up, we want to aspire, we want our world to be ordered and just, thereby giving ourselves an appropriate part in it. We want to know who we are and should be. So where must we look to find this? At someone else? No, not just someone else, everyone else! Everyone who looks at us makes us who we are, and we both need them and hate them for that power. One dissenting voice can totally unmake who we think we are, so our relation to others is a continual politicking to keep our identity in office. Our thumotic desire for justice and rank turns us towards one another in imitation, but the more we turn towards each other the more our anger and rivalry grows along with our needy desperation for meaning.

The more we crave meaning, the more of a mess we become. All of us have something of the proverbial teenager in us who hates and loathes the very ones he is most desperate to impress. Do we loath others first, or ourselves? It is impossible to say. Teenage angst is suicidal, but no less homicidal. We flatter ourselves that we have matured beyond our high school insecurities. But our imaginations prove unable to grow up. Adolescent music and fashion obsess us; both are the default position of what constitutes popular taste. The stories most of us love manifest that we are dreaming collectively about adolescent tribulations and adolescent triumphs.

Take, for example the teenage ritual of "playing chicken."

All of us know the set up, even if we have different names for it. Two teenagers, desperate to impress a girl, race toward each other on a single-

---

This presentation is a two-fold action: action on the part of the other, and action on its own part. In so far as it is the action of the *other,* each seeks the death of the other. But in doing so, the second kind of action, action on its own part, is also involved; for the former involves the staking of its own life. Thus the relation of the two self-conscious individuals is such that they prove themselves and each other through a life-and-death struggle. . . . Similarly, just as each stakes his own life, so each must seek the other's death, for it values the other no more than itself.

*G. W. F. Hegel,* Phenomenology of Spirit, *§187*

lane highway. There must be a girl involved because the issue appears to be erotic. But there is also a crowd, an audience, indicating something else is at work here. As in days of old, this modern-day duel is an affair of honor, and by honor we mean the desire to be looked up to. Unfortunately this also means there must be someone looking down. In the past the vertical ordering of gentlemen and commoners limited duels to those between gentlemen because their willingness to kill or be killed both constituted and presupposed that rank. In high school rank is up for grabs, and the game of chicken reveals its thumotic source. A willingness to be killed and suffer the loss of everything you have or might have—your body, your girl and your car—shows you have risen above the embarrassment of erotic fear for safety, and are willing to gamble it all for thumotic honor and face. How will you win? By the now explicit rather than implied willingness to kill someone wanting the very same thing as you. You must stake your life and take another's to win this struggle for recognition. Both, however, can't win. If neither swerve, they are both dead, and there is no drama, no plot and no honor because the audience required to make this drama work has been killed in the process. For who is worthy to confer the crown of being victor in this game but the someone who was also willing to become victim? Only someone thumotic enough to overcome their own fear of death can serve as model for victory, and yet that very same model must be defeated as a rival if one is to win.

So someone must swerve. There must be a loser for there to be a winner. What the loser loses to is his battle with the erotic fear of death. The winner has overcome that fear, not only by not swerving, but by plowing ahead and proving a willingness to kill as well as be killed. This death-dealer has put death to death, but only on condition that the loser keeps death alive as his mastering fear. There is now an erotic slave and a thumotic master, because both have agreed beforehand that thumos should rule in themselves and in others. The winner gets the girl. The loser gives her to him by fearing an even more precious loss, the loss of his own body. The winner receives this gift on one condition: that the loser's defeat mean much more than winning the girl. What the winner and now master has truly won is not the girl but the loser and slave, whose fearful and upward glance makers the winner who he is and gives him everything he has. The loser and slave thumotically makes the winner and slave everything he now is. Who then is truly master here? Losers define who are the winners; they alone have the power to do so.

The game of chicken makes fearfully manifest what the jockeying for rank in status in high school is all about. At the very time when it is said that our bodies are erotically crazed taking whatever they can get, it turns out that our thumotic hearts are much more engaged in violently receiving who we are in the eyes of others. We are all in a life-or-death struggle for meaning, mastering our identity, even as we slavishly give that power over to those who don't seem to need it as desperately as us. Who are the "cool" kids but those erotically cool and therefore thumotically hot and socially lethal? Everyone knows who the winners and losers are because all have agreed on the ground rules of the suicidal and homicidal game of being part of the "in crowd." Unfortunately, the rules seem to be the same to be part of any crowd at all.

Of course, put on a few more years in college or the working world, and things look quite different. The madness of this crowd has worn off, and the losers, weirdoes and geeks are now in control and an entirely new game

---

The *truth* of the independent consciousness is accordingly the servile consciousness of the bondsman. This, it is true, appears at first *outside* of itself and not as the truth of self-consciousness. But just as lordship showed that its essential nature is the reverse of what it wants to be, so too servitude in its consummation will really turn into the opposite of what it immediately is; as a consciousness forced back into itself, it will withdraw into itself and be transformed into a truly independent consciousness.

G. W. F. Hegel, Phenomenology of Spirit, §193

---

is afoot. Their fears have been internalized through years of servitude, the master is now within rather than without, and the violent competition for meaning now takes place safely in an economic arena of production versus consumption. Long hours and delayed gratification produce the supply of the new winners; premature and overleveraged consumption provides the demand of the new losers. Both, however, now believe in the market as the thumotic arena of meaning, with thumotic competition still making them who they are. Winners need losers, just as losers need winners, but everybody hates this need and so pretends they are who they are independently of anyone else. Our undisguised contempt when we see this need in others is itself the disguise we wear to hide the lethal servitude in ourselves.

Is this, then, the problem, as a Marxist critic might say, that we are disgustingly bourgeois, middle class and capitalist? I think not. No political, cultural or economic system has made us this way. On the contrary, we are the ones making those various systems in order to deal with and survive with the way we are.[1] The thoughts and passions of the human heart make it an actual liar and potential murderer. What are we to expect of the system that governs those hearts, living together? Actual lies and actual murder, systemized.

In the next chapters we will look into this process of political making to see how these actual lies and murders take place. But in the final chapter we will ask the most important question of all: Can we ever change? Is the "desperately wicked" human heart, the defective building block with which we must build our political world of safety and meaning, doomed to remain the same forever?

---

[1]Cf. John Paul II, *On Social Concern / Sollicitudo Rei Socialis: Encyclical Letter of the Supreme Pontiff John Paul II . . . for the Twentieth Anniversary of Populorum Progresso* (Boston: St. Paul Books & Media, 1987), §36-37.

# 4

## WHAT WE DON'T WANT TO SEE

*O Oedipus, God help you! God keep*
*you from the knowledge of who you are!*
SOPHOCLES *OEDIPUS THE KING*

Illusive as the heart may be, we can always catch a glimpse of it in Greek tragedy. Filled with incest, murder, eating of children, cross-dressing and pathological intoxication, these tragedies might seem over-the-top soap operas, bordering on camp. Except for one thing. They are dead serious. As much as we might giggle nervously as we see or read them, we still feel something primordial and profound is at work here. We are filled with a vague dread. The source of this dread—the reason these dramas affect us even when wrenched out of the original political and cultural context of ritualized theater—is that they uncover what we usually seek to hide. Just as the original actors wore masks, what is said and done on stage unmasks something hidden in the audience. And yet as soon as we get this horrifying glimpse of ourselves, the mask of the stage is lowered and hides it again.

Dionysus, the Greek god of theater, rules over the stage and reveals its true function. For this adolescent god, lord of revelry and drunkenness, is also the god of ritualized violence. Torn limb from limb, Dionysus is re-membered again in the cathartic experience of the audience—like a drunken revel in which not a person is sober and in the next instant all are passed out and asleep, Greek theater effects the transition from dismembering orgiastic violence to peaceful and forgetful slumber. As this god and his murderous dismemberment reminds us, lurking behind all great tragedies is the arbitrary victim, or scapegoat, who purges us of our mimetic rivalry.

Yet in addition to this lurking victim, there is also the poetic artifact of the drama itself. What takes place on stage functions as a shareable world that takes up into itself all the unshareable tensions of our erotic and thumotic desires. The tragedy's poetic beauty and charm is itself what gives the pleasant feeling of peaceable unity to its audience, even as it belies whatever violent and painful disunities confront them on stage. What has traditionally been called "catharsis" or purging, is this massive gap between the pleasure in the audience and the pain on stage, as well as the mysterious movement from one to the other. In short, what Greek tragedy *does* in a controlled and politically directed way is what happens when a crowd moves from hatred to calm after a lynching.

In a lynching the victim appears to embody everything the crowd hates and fears in its various rivalries. Likewise, what we see on the tragic stage are all the passions, fears and rivalries that scare the hell out of us when we see them in our neighbor rather than ourselves. Nevertheless, by seeing our fears in all their dark splendor we also seem to get rid of them. We forget them and go on living with one another as though they were not. Greek tragedy thus deceives us even as it tells us the truth.

Initially, Greek tragedy may well seem to solve the riddle of the Sphinx. Lurking outside the city of Thebes, devouring anyone who cannot answer her question, the Sphinx asks "what walks on four legs in the morning, two in the afternoon, and three in the evening?" The answer, of course, is ourselves, through our youth, maturity and age. A wandering Oedipus solves this riddle, ends the plague of the Sphinx, and gets himself made king by marrying the recently widowed queen. Oedipus, it would seem, knows something about who we are.

Nevertheless, at the beginning of Sophocles' *Oedipus the King,* we find that a new plague has come upon the city of Thebes. Oedipus may have become king because he knew what man in general was, but he does not know who he himself is. He does not know that he has killed his father, the old king, and is sleeping with his own mother the old and new queen. The tragic flaw that leads to his downfall is, however, not the doing of either of these things. It is his pursuit of coming to know them. As his own mother and wife Jocasta puts it, "God keep you from the knowledge of who you are!" When in spite of this warning he *does* come to know who he is, he blinds himself. We, the audience, would do the same. We would come to know who we are, yet we must also blind ourselves to live with what we might see. We are not Oedipus, but do we not have our own "Oedipal" truth? If so, what is it?

Incest. Incest and murder. If you are shocked or offended at this accusation, we are on the right track. The feeling of repugnance and anger shows we are in the arena of thumos; and thumos will be our thread to lead us into the strange labyrinthine relations we have to incest. Consider why many anthropologists consider incest the one universal taboo. If I were to naively ask you why you don't consider sleeping with your parents, siblings or children, especially since they are closer to you than anyone else, you would no doubt respond with disgust, horror or at least nervous laughter. If I ask again, "why not?" you may sputter out some claim about birth defects or inbreeding. Is that truly what is going on here? Apart from the accuracy of these biological reasons, if you knew nothing of them you would still recoil at the suggestion—you and almost all of humanity. Were we all born with a special insight into biological inbreeding? Not likely. So what is it then? As even Jocasta says to Oedipus, in dreams and oracles "many a man has lain with his own mother. But he to whom such things are nothing bears his life most easily" (Sophocles *Oedipus the King* 980-984). But why *this* dream, and why the recoil in horror at acting it out?

In one sense we have already answered this. The horror of incest is the horror in facing the implications of our own erotic and thumotic tendencies. Our erotic passion that wants to possess, to eat up and consume everything confronting it, has no intrinsic limits. But our body does. When we consume things they disappear and we must turn elsewhere. Our sexual desires check us even more. Even as they draw us to join with another body, our very bodies guarantee they will never succeed. At the very moment of orgasm, seeming object of desire and height of physical unity, our bodies betray us, recede and fall apart. Yet out of this ephemeral union, a true union can take place in the form of a child, but that unity is radically *not* ourselves. It is a new body, as separated by its own skin as its mother remains separate from its father. Our erotic passion longs to become one with others through possession, but it cannot succeed because the means to that satisfaction are through the body. There can only be union in some third body that is partially of both bodies and yet finally neither.

This fact of unshareable bodies, along with our continued desire to overcome it through the body, is what makes incest taboo. What is prohibited in incest is the attempt, as much as the body can, to satisfy the erotic desire to possess oneself in sameness, to not lose oneself in otherness. And all of this is in spite of the body's merely sexual desire that left to itself will lead to exactly that. If we, like Oedipus, return to our mother's womb during intercourse—are we not trying to give birth again only to ourselves? Bodies, of course, can never be the same, but if we give birth to brothers that are also our sons, or sisters that are also our daughters, or nieces that are also daughters, and so on, our very "blood ties" are ties only to ourselves. We have expanded to encompass even our family into ourselves.

Herein lies the source of the prohibition. If we are only ourselves and our family is only our body writ large, are we not then at war with every other body or family? Would not the very inassimilable nature of every body and every family not of our own blood demand that it be destroyed if it could not be swallowed up into our own? Would not our desire to possess put us at war with otherness itself?

If incest is what the taboo is against, marriage is what it is for. If our bodies cannot be shared erotically, they can at least be shared politically. If the taboo against incest is observed, every marriage must be outside one's own blood. A unity in otherness will be bred into us, both above us in our parents and below us in our offspring. We will then be tied to others through our erotic satisfactions rather than cut off from them. Erotic desire left to itself can go either way. In our dreams, as Jocasta admits, we see what our limitless desires make us capable of. In our "taboos," we experience the fear of what happens if that desire is not checked. The incest taboo is the sleeping fear of our sleeping desires. Awaken either and we have a tragedy on our hands.

The incest of Oedipus, or the many tragic plots involving parents eating or destroying their children, manifest what our erotic desires make us capable of. All of us could be bestial gods who would consume without limit, until, like a giant spider, we have converted the whole world into our own body's blood. Yet we see this safely only in others and on stage. The private fears of the same thing in ourselves remain in our visceral shuddering and the cathartic purging at the very thought.

What we shudder at is blood, both blood spilt and blood inherited. Oedipus hearkens back to our fear of inherited blood. If we are to survive each other we must break free of our voracious selves just as we must break free of our blood ties. In the *Oresteia* by Aeschylus we shudder at blood spilt. For in this play the orgy of blood-letting in the very midst of family brings out the violence that attends upon the coupling of our erotic desires to consume with our thumotic desire for justice. We saw a bit of this already when Oedipus killed his father in a fit of early road rage. In the *Oresteia* we will see that the political landscape of eros and thumos are laid bare in all their complicated interactions.

The "House of Atreus," focal point of the entire *Oresteia* trilogy, is tragically cursed and doomed because Atreus' grandfather, Tantalus, killed and cooked his children before serving them to the gods. Tantalus' punishment in Hades for this deed is the epitome of erotic punishment. Everything he would desire of food and drink is held "tantalizingly" close, but when he moves to have it, it is withdrawn. His grandson, Atreus, has a new twist on the family habit. When his brother revolts from his rule over Thebes, his punishes the now repentant brother by killing, cooking and feeding him his own children in a feast of reconciliation.

We are now well beyond eros and in the thumotic world of vengeance, rivalry and murder. Yet no one can leave behind family. Atreus has a son, Agamemnon, who as king of the Greeks against the Trojans is also married to Clytemnestra. As husband and king, Agamemnon and his familial tragedy is our own, privately as individuals and politically as citizens.

Agamemnon is going to war. Paris committed an injustice against both his brother and all the Greeks by stealing Helen. The Greeks, with Agamemnon as their chief, must take their vengeance. The fleet is ready to sail, but the gods won't let it go without a sacrifice. The victim they demand is Agamemnon's daughter Iphigenia. Now this is rather unusual.

Fathers must forever sacrifice their sons on the altar of war, for such are the thumotic demands of justice and honor. But a daughter? To sacrifice one's daughter is more like devouring one's children as food rather than sacrificing them for justice. But the curse of Tantalus will out, so Agamemnon binds up her mouth to kill her so he cannot hear what we in the tragic audience do not want to see.

The deed is done, the fleet can sail, but Agamemnon's wife, of course, stays home. For ten long years, she farms out the raising of their son Orestes and shacks up with Agamemnon's cousin, Aegisthus, who somehow survived his father's untoward feast. When Agamemnon returns home, Clytemnestra and Aegisthus murder him in his connubial bath, take over the throne, and rule over Thebes. That is, until Orestes will himself return home, goaded by Apollo, and slay both Aegisthus and his own mother. The blood of his own mother on his hands; the Furies now appear to Orestes. Blind, feminine goddesses of thumotic vengeance with dripping, empty eye-sockets, the Furies hound him all the way to Athens, demanding justice. In Athens we get it. The Furies are the prosecuting attorneys; Apollo the Olympian god of light and "civilization" shows up as the defense; and Athena herself is both judge and deciding vote on a jury of ten Athenian citizens.

At stake in this trial is something we have seen in the case of incest, but mixed in now with the distinctly human and political context of thumos. The Furies are furious at Orestes' murder of his mother. This injustice cannot stand because the murder of his own flesh and blood is destruction of that thumotic extension of one's own that we all extend from our own bodies to that of our immediate kin. If we have no fear of killing our own kin, then neither will we have fear of killing anyone else. The primal fear allowing each of us to survive each other with our life and our possessions intact will prove ineffective, leading to chaos and death. The Furies embody the argument of our calculations that fear is the only way we can live with each other in the midst of our private and hidden erotic desires.

And yet the Furies have no concern for the Clytemnestra's murder of Agamemnon. This was not a murder of kin, but only an unrelated spouse. It is therefore not tied in to the problematic "sameness" and unshareability of our own body with its erotic desires and fears. Apollo, however, the newer and political Olympian god has a different concern. Rather than the ancient, feminine and autochthonous concerns of the Furies, his concern is with the murder of a husband and king, and the thumotic demand for justice and honor on the part of a son and heir. The Olympian gods may well have come to power when Zeus defeated his own father, Chronos, but if we blink that fact, as we must, the civilized world of light they represent is a good and necessary thing. Their revolt established a political and vertical ordering, and this new political rather than familial ordering coalesces around the ties of marriage rather than blood. The political ties of marriage depend upon covering over the erotic ties to our own body and mother in order to move towards the father in his role as thumotic model.

The fear of Zeus, rather than the fear of the Furies, is the thumotic fear of not pleasing the modeling father. Even though it is still coupled with the fear of stronger, because institutionalized, force, this fear is fundamentally one of dishonor and shame. The fear of Zeus and his thunderbolts, one might say, is the fear behind the taboo against incest. The irrationality of the fear built into our use of the word *taboo* flows from the fact that it is not our usual erotic and self-interested calculating fear. It is instead the fear flowing from our thumotic need for justice and the ranking it requires.

In the case of marriage, the prohibition against marrying blood relations is the backhanded presence of the political need for a connection between bodies based upon a shareable third—be it marriage to political rather than blood kin, or children who are legitimate rather than natural. The male Agamemnon is thus more tied into marriage than the female Clytemnestra, not because he is male but because he is the man and father as in "man and wife." Our tie to our mother is directly through the body and erotic, but our tie to our father—especially because we do not know for sure he is ours apart from the institution and legitimacies of marriage—is thumotic and political. Give us the political world and its thumos and we have sons and fathers who in turn can become Men, but give us only bodies and eros, and all we have are mothers, daughters and plenty of boys, but no Men.

This would seem to be why Apollo makes his final point that the seed of a child comes not from the mother, who is naught but a holding tank or pot for things to grow in, but from the seed of the man who is the animating and sole source of the child. Apollo and the Greeks were not, I suspect, ignorant of the facts of life. Anyone who has seen the features of a mother on the face of her child knows this cannot be true. Nonetheless this lie is the political lie in its essential form, for it is this lie that creates the seeming shareability of political ties in the face of unshareable blood and bodies. Without this lie and the uncanny fear we still feel before our taboos, there would be no city, marriages, fathers or sons. All that would remain would be monsters, like the Cyclops in Homer's *Odyssey* who lacked both city and laws because they lacked fear of the uncanny gods.

Devouring each other because of our unchecked and monstrously enlarged appetites would be the last word. The reputed hostility against the womb is merely the primal fear before our own devouring eros and hidden

---

They have not meeting place for council, no laws either,
no, up on the mountain peaks they live in arching caverns—
each a law to himself, ruling his wives and children,
not a care in the world for any neighbor.

*Homer* The Odyssey *9.125-128*

---

incestual dreams, dreams that would make all of us, male and female, monstrous gods whose desire to possess goes way beyond the limits of their own bodies.

This is Apollo's brief. Orestes is justified in killing his mother for he is exacting vengeance for her murder of his father, the institution of marriage, and the legitimacy and status of a son. The Furies, on the side of the mother rather than the wife, are arguing for the primordial demands of the body and the primacy of eros over thumos. Who shall win? Both seem to have half of our nature on their side, split up, as it were, into a fundamental battle between the sexes.

Athena casts the deciding vote for Apollo. Female, and yet virginal, sprung from the head of her own father Zeus in apparent confirmation of Apollo's patriarchal case, her very virginity tells of her thumotic ascendancy. For in denying her eros she brings out the political role of thumos. She is under the aegis of her father Zeus, because she is on the side of wives rather than mothers, and on the side of the new and precarious development of the city rather than the old world of the body. Above all, her warlike spear, helmet and shield bespeak her thumotic and warlike ways that are the necessary accouterments of the passion for justice. Still, Athena also stands in for reason, but in her case reason comes out in the form of persuasion backed up by force.

Whether this "reason" is not indeed mere rhetoric, a fraud and lie, is rendered questionable by her agreement with the case of Apollo—women are not our mothers. Her own fabricated status as a goddess is proof of this, but that does not make it any less a lie, even if breathed through the silver of our political needs. The Furies may have lost their case, but they are not happy, and the needs and fears they represent must still be met. How are we to avoid a thumotic world of sterility and death that would result if thumos were fully disconnected from eros and the body? And yet, just as the body and feminine fertility give life, increase and pleasure, disconnect them from the predominately male thumos and their flip side of death, sterility and pain will result.

Athena, in her position as patroness of political founding, must therefore accomplish the subordination of eros to thumos, whereby the life-giving elements of eros are maximized and its death-dealing aspects are minimized. To accomplish this she persuades the Furies that they will be honored in the city, that they will achieve their erotic ends in the higher context of thumotic satisfactions. Children will be tied to legitimacy, and sexuality will be tied to marriage, and even the very increase of the soil will be tied to the political seasons of planting and harvest rather than the random workings of flood and drought.

And if persuasion should not work, Athena always has access to the thunderbolts of her father. For thumotic violence is at root both the problem and the solution. If we were merely erotic we would be animals, and our own bodies would provide us with our solutions. But we are the animal that wants more than eros, we want justice. The essential role of force and fraud therefore seems to be our lot.

Athena finally transforms the malign Furies into the benign Eumenides, giving us both the title of Aesychylus' last play in the trilogy and the archetypal solution to the political problem. If we ask what it is that ultimately persuades the Furies to change, we will be asking ourselves what it is that can transform the thumotic passion for justice into a good rather than an evil. Our clue returns us to the scapegoat. The chorus comments as it witnesses the transformation of the Furies to the side of Athens and its justice: "This is my prayer: Civil War fattening on men's ruin shall not thunder in our city. Let not the dry dust that drinks the black blood of citizens through passion for revenge and bloodshed for bloodshed be given our state to prey upon. Let them render grace for grace. Let love be their common will; let them hate with single-heart. Much wrong in the world thereby is healed" (Aeschylus *The Eumenides* 975-986, Lattimore translation).

Civil war is the fruit of the Furies' vengeance. If everyone is against everyone else, and our ineradicable thumotic nature harnessed to our unlimited eros leads to a war of all against all, then we are doomed politically and economically. Our demand for justice will kill us. But if we can project our desire for justice outward, against an external enemy rather than each other, we might somehow live with our thumotic hatred and passion for justice and yet still love each other. In other words, we need an enemy. And if the enemy does not present himself (for who is primordially our enemy but each other?) we must invent him—hence the scapegoat and the cathartic powers of a lynching. We need our enemies if we are to be friends, because we cannot have our mimetic modeling without rivalry.

The *Oresteia* as the story of the transformation of deadly justice and deadly thumotic passions is also the story of how this deadly rivalry can be transformed into something good by means of lies and deception. It tells us of a resurrection, as it were, from the dark and old gods of private eros and thumos, to the new gods of light and politically shareable eros and thumos. Nevertheless, what effects this resurrection is a lie at every level, whether it is the scapegoating of enemies or the con about origins and conception.

We, as the audience of the play, are the lie's final level. The catharsis we feel as we see the truth about ourselves and yet go home satisfied and pleased, as though we had seen something other than the painful truth, should make us suspicious. If tragedy has the effect, as the tragic poet Agathon describes it, of bringing "Peace among human beings, on the open sea calm and cloudlessness, the resting of winds and sleeping of care" (Plato *Symposium* 197d), then we might think we had all seen a plot about something other than the most disturbing storms in the human soul. But we haven't. We have seen the worst that can be imagined, and yet we come away comforted. It is the comfort of the lie, the comfort of the Dionysian mask, made by poets to give us the apparently shareable world we cannot supply by nature.

If we turn to another Greek tragedy, Euripides' *Bacchae*, we get to see the god of theater, Dionysus, as the main character. This god of intoxication and losing oneself in orgiastic forgetfulness shows up in disguise as an adolescent boy smiling smugly and leading a pack of delirious female groupies called *bacchae*. Recognizing the necessity of wine, forgetfulness and sleep to the everyday toil and strain of humanity, the older men follow this god and join in to worship. Even if Dionysus is not a true god, they say, the city must persuade itself that he is; the "fiction is a noble one" and source of all the city's customs and laws. The elders recognize the lie, and yet co-conspire in the making of it. Without it, things could be worse, and as the play unfolds we see just how much worse they could be.

Agave's son, Pentheus, is king of the city. With no father on the scene to speak of, he is nonetheless king; he has no beard and looks suspiciously like the mask of Dionysus. He has not yet become a man. At the beginning of the play, his mother has run off with the bacchae, and is rumored to be partaking in Dionysus's orgiastic rites that obliterate the differences between human and animal and male and female. Unlike the elders, Pentheus attempts to resist the power of Dionysus with his kingly force, as though this god would submit directly to fear. He arrests Dionysus, but Dionysus destroys the prison with an earthquake and, standing before Pentheus, mocks him. Pentheus orders him to be arrested again, until Dionysus gives him a tempting offer. Would he not like to see what is going on out in the fields with the bacchae? "Yes, he would," he falteringly agrees, falling under the spell of the god. "Then, go, put on a dress and I will make it possible," Dionysus instructs him.

Mesmerized, lisping, wearing a dress, Pentheus is now completely under Dionysus's spell. He sees two suns, and two cities, and Dionysus now looks to him as an animal rather than a god. The warlike, divisive and mimetic rivalry built into us humans has become manifest. Dionysus leads him to the pastoral female orgy, puts him in a tree to see it better, and then points him out to the women. With his own mother, Agave, in the lead, the bacchae spot him, pull him down, and tear him limb from limb. In their own intoxication they take him not for a boy in a dress, but for a wild and predatory animal. At the end of this wild dismemberment, Agave puts her son's head on a pole and marches back into the city triumphant at her prowess as a hunter who can compete with any man. The elders, seeing what she holds on the end of her phallic pole, go into mourning and recollect the parts of their king's body, even while wishing that Agave's present madness would last until she dies, for only then would she "*seem* to have, not having, happiness" (Euripides *Bacchae* 1260).

Would, indeed, that Agave not wake up and see this. But of course she does, and that is what we, the audience, have come to see. Would *we* be happy if we knew this, if it were *our* son's head on the end of our stick, as it were? Or has the playwright done for us what the elders hoped for from Dionysus—provided us with a drug that gives us forgetfulness and oblivion as soon as we see our very worst? But what is our worst that we are seeing here?

One clue is the frenzy of the female bacchae. Their hallucinatory intoxication is with a prepubescent god who must inevitably abandon them to sober wakefulness. Imagine today the screaming groupies of our own pop culture scene, starting with Frank Sinatra and the Beatles and bottoming out in the latest boy bands. Why this frenzy, and why does it affect women more than men? Males who look like boys, or androgynous men with long hair and prating ways seem to provoke it, but why them and not mature men or fathers? The answer, I suspect, is because we are dealing with mothers and pubescent potential mothers. Under Dionysus's spell Agave's son puts on a dress, but under the same spell Agave puts away motherly things and takes on the masculine traits of the hunter and killer—and kills her son. Is this lack of differentiation in the midst of Dionysus's orgy perhaps akin to Oedipus' incest? Oedipus sleeps with his mother and is horrified with the result. Agave, in a sense, sleeps with Dionysus as his groupie, and wakens to a horrifying result.

Perhaps the horror in both is the same temptation, and that temptation is to be sexually aroused by one's own body. In Agave's case, the temptation is to sleep with her own son in the form of the beardless Dionysus she ecstatically follows (remember their eerie resemblance to each other). The sexual excitement of dangerous men and players, who everyone not intoxicated with them knows will both manipulate and abandon their victims, is an arousal at the boy inside of the man. The feminine frenzy of the bacchae would thus be the equivalent of the more masculine desire that leads to incest, the difference arising out of out the differing sexual orientation towards childbirth. What arouses feminine incestual desire is not the man who plays a political role as a potential husband, but the "boy" who arouses as the self-enclosed object of a lover who is also his mother. The "hysterical" behavior of the bacchae linguistically connects us to the womb, but as we saw in the Furies, connection to a womb without connection to the political role of a "Man" makes of sexual desire a solipsistic devouring of otherness that arouses all our fears in the face of unshareability. The lack of differentiation between the sexes is a threat because it destroys the political primacy of marriage, and with it, the shareable thumotic world of ranking and difference. It is this ranking and difference that alone seem to save us from the dangerous quality of eros attached to our thumotic passion for justice.

If we were just animals this would be no problem, or if mothers gave birth to daughters without the sexual need and desire for males, again, no problem. Yet because we are not just animals, and because mothers give birth to boys, the problem of dealing with our thumotic nature attached to our erotic desires is a constant challenge to our continued political existence. Give us a world where boys sexually pursue females only as "players" rather than fathers, and where women are only attracted to these same boys as their own imaginary children, and we will soon find out what will happen to their actual children. They will be devoured by all the other Peter Pans, or the now lost-to-themselves Wendys who follow them, and all future children will end up with their heads on a stick. The sexual and violent pathologies of our own inner cities are merely one current realization of what every Greek feared as an imminent possibility.

So runs our fear, because so run our desires. The *Bacchae* shows us both of them. Our primordial desire—and its attendant fear for ourselves and of each other—is the dismemberment into the private parts of a destroyed body politic. The mask of Dionysus is pulled aside for a minute and we get a peek at what we want and yet fear, and the blood of dismembered parts fills our horizon. When the mask is put back on, the dismembered parts are remembered and the theatrical mask of Dionysus returns us to our body politic with all its parts safely in place. What we have seen is the violent dismemberment of a sacrificial victim and scapegoat that reunifies the perpetrators through that very violence. In the audience, however, it is not the violent murder or its symbolic reenactment that unifies. Instead, the political goal of the Greek Dionysian spectacles is the fabricated unity of the tragedy itself, enacted before an audience, that unifies in the very contrast between its ugly and painful revelations on stage and the beautiful and pleasant appreciation of the audience. Tragic catharsis, underneath it all, is an artful lynching.

In our own day all we have left is a vague sense that something important, scary or just plain weird is going on in these tragedies. All that we may think we see out of the corner of our eye appears historically distant from us, or at best, vaguely reminiscent of our own religious tradition. The Christian tradition is also rather bloody, and it deals in its own way with a violent murder, a son, a seemingly absent father and a mother. Yet this tradition goes on right before our eyes. Lying and deceit is its theme, and yet it claims to have done away with the need for either of them. With murder and blood and a body at its very center, it remains a comedy with a happy ending, not a tragedy at all. It wants to uncover all and hide nothing, and yet still hopes for an entirely different way of living with each other.

# 5

## THE HEART AND PHILOSOPHY

*"Then," he said, "if it's that he cares about, he won't be willing to mind the political things."*

*"Yes, by the dog," I said, "he will in his own city, very much so. However, perhaps he won't in his fatherland unless some divine chance coincidentally comes to pass."*

*"I understand," he said. "You mean he will in the city whose foundation we have now gone through, the one that has its place in speeches, since I don't suppose it exists anywhere on earth."*

*"But in heaven," I said, "perhaps, a pattern is laid up for the man who wants to see and found a city within himself on the basis of what he sees. It doesn't make any difference whether it is or will be somewhere. For he would mind the things of this city alone, and of no other."*

PLATO *REPUBLIC*

*"We are lost, afflicted in only this one way: That having no hope, we live in longing."*

VIRGIL IN DANTE'S *DIVINE COMEDY*

Before we can treat with the Christian tradition, however, we must fill out an earlier attempt to uncover the covering of what is called the "tragic lie." This is the philosophical tradition of Plato and Aristotle, begun, one might say, when the aspiring young tragic playwright Plato encountered the philosopher Socrates and promptly went home and burned all his manuscripts. What this philosopher brought to our aspiring young poet's attention was another sort of desire—higher, more noble, and yet smaller and weaker than the titanic erotic and thumotic desires operative in tragedy. This desire, the operative passion of the philosopher who can only want the wisdom he must forever lack, is the desire to know not just this or that, but everything there is to know, all being and reality, beginning with the being of the philosopher himself.

To know this desire is therefore to know its concrete embodiment in the philosopher, particularly as the philosopher finds himself surrounded by the occlusion of knowledge we find in the city. The question of the philosopher and the city is therefore the question writ large of how any-

---

"Won't we also then assert that the philosopher is a desirer of wisdom, not of one part and not another, but of all of it?"

"True.". . .

"But the one who is willing to taste every kind of learning with gusto, and who approaches learning with delight, and is insatiable, we shall justly assert to be a philosopher, won't we?"

*Plato* Republic *475b-d*

---

one's desire to know stands in relation to their desire to be seen and their desire to have. We can see this most clearly if we turn to what Plato wrote instead of a tragedy, his dialogue on both the philosopher and the city he calls *The Republic*.

In it, the character Socrates divides the soul and the city into three parts that correspond to the three desires we have been looking at. The first part corresponds to eros, or the desire to have and keep, that finds its locus in the human body as the chief and ineradicable locus of private property. All of us have "an irrational love of one's own" because we start off by loving our own body above all else. The second desire is thumotic, and, as we have already seen, constitutes the desire for justice and the

consequent spirited passion to kill or be killed in service to whatever un-
reflective notion of justice we happen to inherit from our political world.
In contrast to much modern thought, we are naturally political according
to both Plato and Aristotle because we are naturally thumotic. As much as
we desire to possess and keep, we also desire what is "right," whatever that
"right" might be, and however much that "right" brings us into outright
conflict with everyone else's "right."

This thumotic part of the soul is why we are political, but it is also
at the heart of the political problem. This leads us to our third part and
passion, our desire to know. Because we humans naturally have speech,
or *logos*, whenever we get together with our mix of erotic and thumotic
desires, we not only do things to satisfy those desires, we must also talk
about and justify why we are doing what we are doing. Because our deeds
are always accompanied by words, there is always the latent presence of
the desire to know in all of us, even if only to know what we are constantly
talking about.

By organizing the human soul and his "city in speech" into these three
desires or parts, Plato elucidates the organizing principle between them,
the political concern par excellence, the question of rule or order. In any
decision about what to do or how best to live our life, we must decide
among a myriad of possibilities, and the different desires and fears in each
of us direct us towards or away from different courses of action. Likewise,
in any political decision different types of people within that group desire
and fear different courses of political action depending upon the fears
and desires that have come to rule in them individually. Who is to decide? And yet someone or something must. We must act and so we must
choose. This is the question of rule and the question of order, and as much
as our romantic selves might tend to think otherwise, these questions, not
to mention their answers, are unavoidable.

If we start with the fears and desires of eros, we can see how this starts
to work. Eros wants to have and keep, and it fears to lose. There are a
thousand and one things we have or could lose, but the locus of all this
possession and loss is the private property of our own body. If we put the
manifold erotic desires and fears with the manifold desires and fears of
thumos, we begin to see the issue of rule. Thumos, because of its strange

appetite for justice and how it thinks things should be, finds itself more than capable of subordinating the fears and desires of eros to its own. It enforces that subordination through its willingness to kill other bodies or be killed itself in pursuit of its "justice."

Because of their differing desires and fears, thumos seems designed by nature to rule over eros, if only because it can. But should it? Thumos is that in us that even cares about the answer. Thumos takes up arms in defense of answers to questions like these, questions of what *should* or *ought* to be. Because of its cares, thumos is amenable to being ruled by something above and higher than itself—something that does not rule it extrinsically as thumos does eros, through fear and force, but intrinsically through thumos's own desire for justice. Built into thumos, because of its desire for justice and justifying itself, is a desire to be ruled by and serve something that satisfies a passion and appetite that is not exactly its own—the desire to *know* rather than serve what truly *is* just or right or, at least, should be.

In other words, the desire to know what justice truly *is* is different from the desire to serve or be loyal to that justice. Nevertheless, there is a natural relation of ruler and ruled between the desire to know and the desire to serve. The unarmed pursuit of knowledge can naturally rule over the "arms" that desire to kill or be killed in defense of that knowledge. Like a huge mastiff who might overrule its master through its strength alone and yet loyally desires only to serve, thumos is that middle part of the human soul whose strength designs it to rule over eros, even as its passions design it to serve a weaker and yet natural master. That master is our logos or reason that desires to know the truth of how things should be and what we should do.

The question of political rule or order, in this sense, answers itself. For who or what else should rule than that part of our soul and those few people who are concerned about this very question? This is why Plato's character Socrates argues that the ideal political regime would be ruled by a philosopher-king, who would in turn rule the trained and armed guardians, who would then rule the unarmed multitude of craftsmen and money-makers. So the nature of the parts of our souls would indicate. We are designed to be ruled by knowledge.

The desire to know, with its respective fear of ignorance and deceit, should rule over all other desires and fears. In all other desires fear inevitably begins to predominate, thereby guaranteeing the eclipse of the original desire. The erotic desire to have leads to the fear of loss. The thumotic desire for justice leads to the fear of suffering injustice without getting revenge. Only in the desire of logos, where the fear of ignorance merely restates the desire to know, are our fears and desires in complete harmony. The only way to finally be ruled by desire is to be ruled by the desire to know. Deceit and lies, wherein the fear of loss or dishonor trumps the desire to know, display the essential disorder of the soul wherein these two fears end up dominating the desire to own or be honored.

When the *Republic* tells the story of Socrates' founding his ideal political and psychic regime in speech, it is nevertheless as much an account of the absence of knowledgeable rule in the city as its presence. As much as we might know that this regime is how things ought to be in our soul or in a city, the fact that we must ask how things *ought* to be in the face of what *is,* implies that there is always some other part of the soul and city ruling rather than logos. The fact that we must uncover this fact through questioning reveals that it is a truth that lies hidden, hidden to ourselves and hidden before others. The argument of Plato is that the desire to know, rather than ruling us as it should, is always being turned into some sort of slave or lackey that serves various thumotic or erotic desires as their paid or coerced propagandist. Our desires are disordered, and the desire to know this or any other truth is usually only used in service of our need to lie. By exploring why and how we lie, Plato seeks to reveal what we have lost even as we use what remains.

Consider the implications of Socrates' fully developed "city in speech." Central to the connection between the philosopher-kings and the warrior guardians is the "noble lie" that will convince the thumotic class to love the "body politic" as if it were their own body private. By getting these warriors to love the city as if it were their own body, they will become like tame dogs that will hate other cities as enemies even as they love everyone in their own city as friends. Central to this lie is something true coupled with something patently false. The falsity is the claim that all of them were born in the soil of the city and that it is their common womb. The truth is that none of them will know their true mother, because in the city thus envisioned they will be separated from their mother at birth and raised in common nurseries, barracks and mess halls.

The point of this lie is the same issue we have seen in the Greek tragedies. If people are to live together in a city they must believe they have something in common that is not tied into the flesh and blood of their own family and bloodline. They must think of themselves like Athena, born out of the political womb of their fatherland, rather than out of the private and privatizing womb of their mother. The mother, in this sense, is more tied into the private erotic fears and desires of our own body, whereas the father, because we (and he) only "know" he is our father through the political imagination and the reinforcement of it strictures, is tied into the thumotic world of seeing and being seen.

What this lie means relative to the parts of the soul is that in the absence of being ruled by true knowledge, thumos will take as its criteria for knowledge what is good for its erotic desires. Nevertheless, because it is thumos, it will not only believe what it wants is "right," it will fight thumotically for the justice of getting what eros tells it that it wants. As opposed to being ruled from the top down, with logos at the top, the lie will always reverse this order with eros secretly calling the shots, armed with thumos, while using the covering lies of words and rhetoric. This covering, as we will later see in the Bible, is nonetheless necessary; for even in its captivity and servitude only logos can give whatever shareability we can muster to live together with our unshareable eros.

If we look simply at the element in the city who should rule, the philosopher-king, we see a similar problem. The philosopher-king, who is ruled by the passion to know everything and is thus fit to rule the city because the object of his desire, everything, can be shared in by everyone, is nevertheless not likely to rule any city anywhere because he does not want to rule in the first place—he wants to know. Implied in the *Republic*'s famous "allegory of the cave" is that the philosopher would only become a king and descend into the cave of human politics if he were *compelled*. The city is a cave because the shadows of lying are ineradicable, and however noble the lies of a philosopher-king may be, the city remains a cave. The philosopher as an embodied human being has no desire to do what he is nevertheless compelled to do, and what compels him are the political needs arising from that very body. His particular body remains a residual and ultimately unshareable bond chaining him to everyone else.

In another dialogue Plato calls the self-knowledge required of the philosopher the "art of dying" (*Phaedo* 63e-67e). Among other things, this art implies that the philosopher can only live in the world of shareable and universal being if he abstracts from the particular political situation that arises from his unshareable and yet living body. The desire to know what *is* would seem to remain just that, a mere desire, whose possible satisfaction lies somewhere on the other side of his particular thumotic and erotic desires.

All the various implications in Plato's dialogues of the philosopher's relation to the city seem to converge upon the paradoxical truth that as much as humans must understand themselves politically by relating their ruling to knowledge, what little knowledge is had we see only in appearances and possess only in desire. If the highest human wisdom is to "know we do not know" (*Apology of Socrates* 37e-38e) and the greatest good is to question what virtue is rather than act virtuously (38a), then humanity would seem best defined by a loss and a desire for something we *do not have* and *are not*. Further, *what we are* and *what we do have* would stand in the way of satisfying our most self-defining desire. Who shall untie for us this knot of human existence that remains even at the heights of human excellence?

In Plato, the paradoxical, elliptical and elusive quality of his dialogues mirror in themselves the paradoxical relation of the desire for wisdom to the rest of our desires and fears, just as they mirror the philosopher's relations to the deceitfully corporate desires and fears of the city. To speak of our desire to know we must not only do it negatively by speaking of our lack and want, but we must also discuss its concrete unsatisfiability given the political nature of our human condition. We are indeed political in nature. Yet to see what that means we must keep two things in mind at once: that we must lie and deceive ourselves in order to live together—even as we know we should not and that it is not finally good to do so. Like someone born chronically ill, we are strangely related to health (as indicated by the oddity of the philosopher) as long as we are still alive. If we were to die it would rescue us from sickness and leave only the notion of health, but it would not be ours or our own body's, but only the idea and general condition that invisibly sustained us as long as we were alive. By using the paradoxical structure of the dialogues (rather, as we shall see, than the narrative sequence and directionality of the biblical Fall), Plato positions knowledge and its desired object as continually with us, even as we, for the most part, turn away and lie to ourselves about it. The desperation of our "wickedness," the need to lie and be lied to, like the thrashings of a fever, are the sign in both that we are designed and ordered for something else.

But this is Plato, after all. Notoriously illusive and elliptical, his dialogues may well invite a biblical projection to fill in the blanks of our own ignorance. That might well be. But what if we could see something similar in the relatively dry and pedantic Aristotle? For as much as Plato's dialogues demand that we join in as partner in an ongoing conversation, the schematic and didactic nature of Aristotle's treatises demand that we bring to them the questions that will open up his "answers" in their political and philosophical fullness. Rather than working our way up to the political problem of the philosopher and the city as Plato does, Aristotle works back from it, as it were, schematically laying out a philosophically understood account of human action and ethics—leaving us to detect the fault lines embedded within. But fault lines there are, and what opens at our feet is the same political problematic we see in both Plato and will see in the Bible.

Starting with the preeminence of knowledge and thinking in all the practical decisions leading to the ethical making of who we are, Aristotle orders all this deliberation to the goal of happiness—with happiness defined as "that for the sake of which" we do everything else (*Nicomachean Ethics* 1097a17-18). Notice here that "happiness" is not a feeling; it is rather a goal that can only be found as a known answer to the question. "Why am I doing everything I do in life?" If we can answer, "I am doing everything I do for the sake of this X" we can know this is in fact happiness because we never find ourselves saying we are happy for the sake of something else. Happiness, whatever it is, seems to be the end or goal of all our actions that we *do* know something about, even if we invariably fail to attain it. In this sense it functions like the desire to know that guides us in our questioning, however rarely it is ever satisfied.

Like the desire to know, happiness as a lack, appetite or desire tells us a lot about or own deceptions, mistakes and self-delusions. First of all, it brings out the fact that happiness, in spite of our overwhelming linguistic and behavioral tendencies, is not a pleasure or any other sort of feeling. Even at the height of our most intense or extended feelings of pleasure, we can still ask ourselves *why* we want to feel this way, and must then answer to ourselves with the answer (and not the unspeaking feeling itself) that we are feeling this feeling for the sake of happiness. Or not. The crack-head who lights his pipe and feels his rush, knows full well he is not happy in spite of those feelings. Unfortunately this knowledge and self-awareness appear to be his enemy and threaten to take away what little contentment he has. The last thing the crack-head (or any other addict for that matter) wants to pay attention to is knowledge rather than feelings. Self-knowledge seems only to make the gnawing lack all the greater.

Deep down, most of us agree with the crack-head. We unthinkingly take happiness to be a feeling, as though we were animals with no speech; we forget that we must always "tell" ourselves, in however degraded a way, the *answer* that our feelings are what constitute happiness. But answers are not feelings. Our need to "tell" ourselves notifies us, if we pay attention, that we are telling ourselves a lie. As in the political soul of Plato, we use answers as slaves to serve the commands given by our desires to have and keep our feelings.

One price we pay for this particular self-delusion (especially given our modern democratic tendencies) is we no longer see as clearly that our true situation and problem is that we are thumotic as well as erotic. Despite all our chatter about sensitivity, we are not mere feelers; we are above all actors—actors who must act with and before others on the political stage of seeing and being seen. Aristotle captures this situation with his dual definition of human beings as both the "political animal" and the "animal with speech" (*Politics* 1253a3; *Nicomachean Ethics* 1097b8-12, 1098a3-7). As political, almost all our speaking to ourselves and with each other is engaged in convincing others and ourselves that what we do and how we act is the right way to act. Why is it right? Erotically we answer that those actions make us feel good or at least avoid pain. Thumotically, the answer most congruent with action itself is that such actions are admirable and lead to being praised by others or at least avoiding blame.

Starting with childhood, we are taught to feel pain or forego pleasure for the sake of praise and looking good in the eyes of our parents. Such training raises us to be actors rather than erotic feelers, and those who do not learn to act, or behave, we throw in jail to protect ourselves from them. If we, with Aristotle, pay attention to action rather than feelings, the terms we must pay attention to are the ones we consistently use only when it comes to sports or musical training, terms like "habituation," "virtue" and "character." From the "no pain, no gain" mantra of the sports world, to the refined world of musical virtuosos, we can see that in a world wherein excellence or mediocrity are made manifest on a public stage, the rare ones worthy of praise have spent long hours transforming their actions from deliberate and awkward repetitions to fluid and spontaneous acts that flow from them as a second nature.

This second nature is what Aristotle calls "character" or *ethos*, and it is this character, when applied to living a life rather than playing a sport or instrument, that constitutes the subject of his *Nicomachean Ethics*. If we pay attention to our lives as the sum total of our actions and consider the possibility that happiness is not feeling pleasure or avoiding pain, but is instead acting well and achieving a truly praiseworthy character, then the terms we will use and pay attention to are *virtue* and *vice*. Virtue or excellence defines those actions that are worthy of praise because they are beautiful and noble, whereas vice defines those actions that are worthy of blame because they are base and ugly. In this light, a life of happiness would be a life wherein one has achieved the established character whereby one habitually and constantly acts excellently in the thousand and one concrete actions that make up who we are before others.

This is not to say that Aristotle is concerned with questions of thumos to the exclusion of eros. On the contrary, he is well aware that most people most of the time measure their happiness in terms of pleasure and pain. At the same time, he is also aware that the entire program of ethical education consists in training ourselves and our children to feel pleasure and pain in the thumotically "right" way. What is this right way? What are, as Aristotle puts it, "natural" pleasures, as opposed to "unnatural" pleasures?

Are they not both pleasures pure and simple, with no discrimination apart from their relative intensity?

They would be, if we were just unspeaking and instinctive animals—but we are not. We have speech and are thumotically political, so the question of true pleasure haunts our youth from the very first time we feel guilt sinking our teeth into a stolen cookie. How, then, are we to measure or evaluate a "natural" pleasure if there is nothing to say about the pleasure other than it is pleasurable? Are we to look outside at others' evaluations and therefore alienate ourselves from our feelings as our romantic culture warns us against? Not at all.

What Aristotle reminds us of is that all feelings are connected to and attendant upon our actions. Pain slows us down and makes an action harder to go through with, while pleasure enhances and quickens our readiness to do an action again. Actions as opposed to the feelings they are always connected with are what can therefore be evaluated. They can be judged as right or wrong, good or bad, virtuous or vicious. The feelings that attend upon those actions can in this way constitute a pleasure or pain that is natural or unnatural—natural if the *actions* are truly worth doing and

---

In most men, pleasant acts conflict with one another because they are not pleasant by nature, but men who love what is noble derive pleasure from what is naturally pleasant. Actions which conform to virtue are naturally pleasant, and, as a result, such actions are not only pleasant for those who love the noble but also pleasant in themselves. The life of such men has no further need of pleasure as an added attraction, but it contains pleasure within itself. We may even go so far as to state that the man who does not enjoy performing noble actions is not a good man at all.

*Aristotle* Nicomachean Ethics *1099a10-18, Ostwald translation*

---

unnatural if they are not. In fact, if the desire is for the action rather than the attendant feeling, one can almost guarantee that that feeling, if pleasurable, will be a natural pleasure because of our desire to *do* rather than *feel.* Likewise, if we want only the feeling and have no intrinsic desire for the action that leads to it (injecting a drug for the high, say) we have a sure example of an unnatural pleasure. The unnaturalness lies in the alienation from our own doing and acting, wherein what we do, and consequently, who we are, is merely a tool and slave to serve our feelings.

Reverting back to the child with the stolen cookie, we can now see that the goal of raising a child aright is to get him to feel pleasure from deeds that he knows are right rather than from deeds he knows are wrong. If the child feels this kind of pleasure, praise would not be extrinsic and a reward for the doing, but intrinsic and as desirable as the deeds if unseen and unrewarded. The pleasure, the reward, is simply in the doing of it. Then and only then, would the acting of this child-become-a-man be the same on the outside and the inside, and would truly constitute who he is. Then and only then, would Gyges' ring of invisibility have no effect upon the wearer. Then and only then, would such a man be truly virtuous.

If the object of our attention should be the actions done and the character of the actors rather than their feelings, what actions are the right ones to be done and how are we to come to know them? To answer we must return to the paradoxical absence and yet need for knowledge that we find in Plato and the Bible. In Aristotle, the nature of habituation and the development of a steady character that acts excellently and well requires that we learn what to do by imitation. We must find someone who is already excellent and do what that character would do. Since actions are concrete, particular and relative to ever-changing situations, one can only learn to do such things by observing, internalizing and imitating someone who already knows how to do them. Yet how do we know whom we should imitate, and who is truly excellent at what they are doing, especially when that excellence is not just the outside doing but also the inside feeling in relation to that doing?

If someone acts well, and yet does not enjoy it and does it only out of fear or desire for a reward, then such an action is not virtuous. Unfortunately we cannot discern this from the outside. If we imitate such a one it will not lead to excellence, for our model brings a defect along with him and introduces a flaw in our imitating that cannot be detected apart from another nondefective model. But what if all our models were defective?

How could we attain the desired goal, and how could we know what was desirable in the first place?

Here, in his own way, Aristotle brings out the problem built into our "knowing" and the lack thereof. All of us seem to know enough about human excellence in acting to know what virtue would look like relative to habituation and character. We can know the function of human nature enough to know what being an excellent human would be; and yet, built into that very nature is the condition that becoming excellent does not depend upon such knowledge. Instead, becoming virtuous is radically dependent upon the concrete situation of those whom we are surrounded by and must imitate. The fact that we are political animals means that our concrete political situation, for better or worse, will have more effect upon determining who we will become than any pre- or transpolitical knowledge of our nature. We may be the animal with reason, but because we are also the political animal we cannot talk or know our way to excellent action apart from our political existence with other people.

This chicken-or-egg problem in Aristotle, whereby there must already exist a virtuous model to learn to be virtuous oneself, brings out a tension and paradox in Aristotle that corresponds to Plato's paradoxical relation of the philosopher to the city. Even as it highlights the possibility, if not the contingent fact, that there are no virtuous men in any concrete city (because there would be no virtuous men in the past to imitate), it also reiterates the paradoxical standpoint of the philosopher who can know what virtue is in the abstract even if he cannot enter in upon it in his concrete, bodily political existence.

Not that the philosopher is any less interested in virtue than anyone else. On the contrary, he is decidedly interested in virtue, its nature, cause and so forth; but this also seems to imply the philosopher is more interested in what virtue is than being virtuous himself. Again, as Socrates argues before being put to death by the city of Athens, the only life he considers worth living is not exactly being virtuous, but rather "to converse about virtue" (Plato *Apology of Socrates* 38a). In this sense Aristotle's "theoretical man," as the functional equivalent of Plato's philosopher, would be after the theoretical rather than the active virtues of the "practical man," especially in this very treatise, *Nicomachean Ethics*, of what the virtues are and how they are attained.

Between these two men, the theoretical and the practical, and their respective lives, there arises the question of which life is more excellent. If we can answer this question we are that much closer to answering which life is the best life, the happy life. Asking after the best life is akin to asking after the best regime, but the answer in Aristotle is similar to the answer in Plato—with the same implications. Aristotle will say that the contemplative and theoretical life is the best, for even at its best the political life is but a means to the end of knowing, in the same way that war is for the sake of peace. Implicit in this answer is the question whether the practical life contains within itself the conflictual situation of war. It also indicates that asking after the good life has priority over the thumotic living out of an answer.

Nevertheless, this answer remains problematic for Aristotle. Reason and speech and the objects they pursue are the highest things in us and

---

Therefore, if we take as established (1) that political and military actions surpass all other actions that conform with virtue in nobility and grandeur; (2) that they are unleisurely, aim at an end, and are not chosen for their own sake; (3) that the activity of our intelligence, inasmuch as it is an activity concerned with theoretical knowledge, is thought to be of greater value than the others, aims at no end beyond itself, and has a pleasure proper to itself—and pleasure increases activity; and (4) that the qualities of this activity evidently are self-sufficiency, leisure, as much freedom from fatigue as a human being can have, and whatever else falls to the lot of supremely happy man; it follows that the activity of our intelligence constitutes the complete happiness of man. . . . However, such a life would be more than human. A man who would live it would do so not insofar as he is human, but because there is a divine element within him. This divine element is as far above our composite nature as its activity is above the active exercise of the other [i.e. practical] kind of virtue.

*Aristotle* Nicomachean Ethics *1178a16-30, Ostwald translation*

---

so deserve to rule, and rule most excellently. But their part in us is also divine, and when it rules us we are almost like gods and no longer human. Because this best life is more divine than human, we can't seem to live the best life politically and practically as the mere mortals we are. Nevertheless we cannot put off the demand to think this best life even if that very thinking reveals how far we are from it. Knowing that we don't know, knowing that we aren't virtuous, knowing the truth of our political tensions and lying—this paradoxical knowledge of the philosopher would seem to be the best thing in life. Yet it would still only be best for a philosopher if he were fully divine and a god—but he is not. He is a human, after all, and must live not as a god, but as a frail and political human being who is stuck in the concrete appearances of his given city.

Where does this leave us, but in the same situation of the philosopher's relation to the city as a cave? He can't live happily in the city, but he can't

---

That the city is both by nature and prior to each individual, then, is clear. . . . One who is incapable of participating or who is in need of nothing through being self-sufficient is no part of a city, and so is either a beast or a god.

*Aristotle* Politics *1253a25-30*

---

remain a human outside of it. Aristotle formulates this by saying only a god or a beast can live outside the city.

Excellence is a demand and happiness is our desire, but because we must know what excellence is and what happiness is in order to possess either, all we have of either is our impoverished longing for them. And yet that very longing and lack seems to be our greatest wealth.

All this relative wealth, however, is only from the standpoint of the philosopher. From within the typical concrete city, wherein virtue is rarely if ever a goal, and most people most of the time pursue their erotic desires and fears, we are dealing with the situation that we have seen in the Greek tragedies. Aristotle describes this situation in his *Poetics* and his *Rhetoric* as the contrast between the respective fears of the philosopher and the virtuous man—being ignorant and being unjust—and the dominant fears of everybody else: the fear of suffering an injustice (*Rhetoric* 1382a20-25). The prevailing political situation is therefore one in which we look to other people for our "happiness" or "goodness," both of which consist finally in the avoidance of pain. The dominant emotion we bear towards others is fear, or at best pity; but both are calculative and painful emotions that look to ourselves and others solely in terms of suffering injustice. Sooner or later these self-serving emotions will blow apart the appearances that unify the city, so they must be purged. In Greece this purging was the catharsis of tragedy that puts on stage our painful fears and leaves the audience with the illusion of pleasant unity. It is, of course, a lie, a *pharmakon*, and a drug, but Aristotle has no harsh words for it in his works on poetry and rhetoric as it seems necessary for the many in actual cities to even live together.

Nevertheless, as Aristotle knows full well, it remains that catharsis has nothing to do with happiness, truth or virtue—which is to say, our becoming good human beings. We are, it seems, destined for more. Yet in Plato and Aristotle there is no more. If we are alive, in a city, and a mere mortal, we can be good apparently or partially, but not fully or truly. Goodness, in truth, must be found elsewhere.

# 6

## THE KNOWLEDGE OF
## GOOD AND EVIL

*"Know ye not me? . . . Not to know me argues yourself unknown."*

SATAN IN MILTON'S *PARADISE LOST*

How, then, are we to be good in the face of our deceitful heart? Will knowledge—above all, self-knowledge—do us any good? Even in the philosophical heights of Socrates' and Aristotle's theoretical lives, self-knowledge seems to reach its limits in the gap between knowing and being virtuous, the gap between the need to live in a city with our bodies public and private and the truly shareable objects of desire that are only above and beyond those bodies. The self-knowledge of Socratic political philosophy would seem to be that there must always be a cave, even the cave of the city in speech, and however much a philosopher's desire to know may lead him into the sunlight, self-knowledge requires he also know his inextricable bodily and political bondage to the shadow world of erotic and thumotic desire.

The theoretical life of Aristotle's description is a life of peace and happiness and is divine rather than human, but we remain at war in practice and unhappily alive with our human, all-too-human, erotic and thumotic desires. As much as erotic desires on their own push forward to their natural limitation by thumotic arms and discipline, and thumotic desires push forward toward obedience to a higher desire and master, the desire to know that could harmonize and integrate all other desires faces a

paradoxical frustration in fact if not in theory. This is the comic paradox
of philosophical self-knowledge, comic because it does indeed know, but
paradoxical because what it knows is the lie of our political selves usually
covered over in tragedy. The life lived out of this self-knowledge must
needs be one of resignation because there is nothing to be done about it.

---

For the beginning of philosophy as the philosophers understood it
is not the fear of the Lord, but wonder. Its spirit is not hope and fear
and trembling, but serenity on the basis of resignation.

*Leo Strauss, "On the Euthyphron," in* Rebirth of Classical Rationalism,
*p. 206*

---

The city and the cave remain, no matter the few who may periodically
escape it. So, again, the question remains: what good is this knowledge
when it comes to ourselves ? Can it lead to us becoming good, practically
and humanly? Can we truly integrate our erotic and thumotic desires with
our desire to know? Can we ever share our erotic and thumotic satisfactions the way we share the objects of knowledge?

We can, I believe and I hope, but we must first take a look at our desire to know and approach it in a different way. To do so we must tell a
story, but we can at least argue why we need to do so. What if our desire
to know had as it object not the erotic whole described by Socrates, nor
the unmoved mover of Aristotle who moves all others through desire, but
rather had as its object a person like ourselves who made that whole and
thereby stands apart from it as creator to creature.

Such an object of desire changes our desire to know. It now becomes
personal. Our desire to know cannot know itself apart from the Person
that elicits that desire, and Whom we desire, when we desire to know,
changes our relation to all our other erotic and thumotic desires. True self-
knowledge could thus only be had from without, from the standpoint of
whom we seek, and not from within our own desiring. In short, the truth
about ourselves would have to be told to us, especially if the truth we are
seeking is indeed a Who, who like ourselves, can communicate himself.

And won't we also then assert that the philosopher is a desirer of wisdom, not of one part and not another, but of all of it? . . . But the one who is willing to taste of every kind of learning with gusto, and who approaches learning with delight, and is insatiable, we shall justly assert to be a philosopher, won't we?

*Plato* Republic *474b-c*

And since what is in motion and causes motion is something intermediate, there is also something that causes motion without being in motion, which is everlasting, an independent thing, and a being-at-work. But what is desired and what is thought cause motion in that way: not being in motion, they cause motion. . . . But the power of thinking is set in motion by the action of the thing thought. . . . And it causes motion in the manner of something loved, and by means of what is moved moves other things.

*Aristotle* Metaphysics *1072a20-1072b5*

Is there such a telling out there, a story of our desire to know as told from the goal of all our seeking? I believe there is. It is the biblical story of the Fall. It is a story told from the vantage point of knowledge lost, that can speak of the frustrations of our desire to know only in relation to our past and a satisfaction of that desire only in relation to our future, As to our present, what the philosophers describe as our nature can only be told of as an ongoing relation to another person, the personal God of Abraham, Isaac and Jacob—and as we shall see, Jesus.

Before we can retell ourselves this story, we must distinguish it from another story. This is the story of the "Romantic" Fall. Designed to sound like the biblical Fall, it nevertheless is designed to supplant it and replace its emphasis on knowledge through the creator God, with something that is hostile to the very desire to know itself. Both start from the same troubling tendencies we have already seen with respect to our thumos and crazy appetite for justice. Both explain how we have fallen into this world of lies and deceit. But where we fell from, and what that means for what we are now, is radically different. Let me sketch out one account and see how it works.

Long ago we lived in a garden of delights as free, innocent and solitary animals, at one with nature, with no self-consciousness. Like children, what we now call our "inner child" was then "outer," and our erotic desires were straightforward and unburdened by the thumotic pressures of looking and being looked at by one another. Because our inner selves were the same as our outer selves, there was no need to hide or cover ourselves, so we strode about naked and revealed. Unfortunately this state couldn't last,

---

I answer that, It was necessary for man's salvation that there should be a knowledge revealed by God besides philosophical science built up by human reason. Firstly, indeed, because man is directed to God, as to an end that surpasses the grasp of his reason: "The eye hath not seen, O God, besides Thee, what things Thou hast prepared for them that wait for Thee" (Isaiah 66:4). But the end must first be known by men who are to direct their thoughts and actions to the end. Hence it was necessary for the salvation of man that certain truths which exceed human reason should be made known to him by divine revelation. Even as regards those truths about God which human reason could have discovered, it was necessary that man should be taught by a divine revelation; because the truth about God such as reason could discover, would only be known by a few, and that after a long time, and with the admixture of many errors. Whereas man's whole salvation, which is in God, depends upon the knowledge of this truth. Therefore, in order that the salvation of men might be brought about more fitly and more surely, it was necessary that they should be taught divine truths by divine revelation. It was therefore necessary that besides philosophical science built up by reason, there should be a sacred science learned through revelation.

*Thomas Aquinas* Summa Theologica *1.1 q. 1*

---

for if we were to gain knowledge and grow up into the social and deceit-ful adults we now are, we must lose this innocence and gain the troubling burdens of responsibility, even if at the expense of losing our freedom and straightforward nudity. So we fell—from innocence to knowledge, from

---

It is, however, an astounding thing that the mystery furthest from our ken, that of the transmission of sin, should be something with-out which we can have no knowledge of ourselves.

Without doubt nothing is more shocking to our reason than to say that the sin of the first man has implicated in its guilt men so far from the original sin that they seem incapable of sharing it. . . . Certainly nothing jolts us more rudely than this doctrine, and yet, but for this mystery, the most incomprehensible of all, we remain incomprehensible to ourselves. The knot of our condition was twisted and turned in that abyss, so that it is harder to conceive of man without this mystery than for man to conceive of it himself.

*Blaise Pascal,* Pensées, *p. 65*

---

freedom to servitude, from unhampered and peaceful eros to competitive and manipulative thumos. Sound familiar? You bet it does. Where does it come from? If you say the Bible, you couldn't be more wrong.

What you have just heard is the myth of Fall in Romanticism. For-mulated initially and most persuasively by Rousseau, it has grown in the telling until we cannot hear of "gardens" and living "east of Eden" without thinking of Woodstock and people over thirty.

This fall was indeed a fall into knowledge and self-consciousness, but the reason we blush for shame at the memory of it is that this "knowl-edge" was the knowledge of power and control that could only know things through dissection and manipulation. It was not the knowledge that let things "be." According to this Romantic telling, if there is to be any escape from the alienating ravages of this knowledge, it must come through the poetic return to nature we find in word or song or utopian politics (cf. John Lennon's song "Imagine").[1]

All those alienated and "happy" with this fall into knowledge align themselves on the side of business, science and consumption, but all those unhappy with it align themselves on the side of creative self-expression in the arts. Most, however, find themselves split right down the middle, working in the adult world during the week and the day to keep money in their pockets, while living in the other world at night and on weekends where their true and nearly forgotten individual selves come out and play like children.

As antidote to the "bourgeois self" we have described earlier (the one who thinks only of himself when it comes to what he wants and yet thinks only of others when it comes to who he is), the "Romantic self" seeks to overcome this selfish and social alienation by moving to the self-contained and yet nonselfish expression of some sort of art: be it dance, music, song

---

Almighty God, you who hold minds in your hands, deliver us from the enlightenment and the deadly arts of our fathers, and give back to us ignorance, innocence, and poverty—the only goods that can bring about our own happiness and that are precious in your sight.

*Jean-Jacques Rousseau,* Discourse on the Arts and Sciences, *p. 19*

---

or the internal phantasmagoria of drugs. There is no going back in this sort of Fall, so we must go forward—forward into the brave new world of increasing freedom *from* knowledge as manipulation and into freedom *for* self-expression.

The more or less implicit argument in all this is that whatever deceit we may find in ourselves comes from the influence upon us of others, and if we were just left to ourselves we would become whole again and pose no threat to ourselves or others. The self we express in our play is our deep-down good and only appears to be evil because of our fall into the baleful influences of trying to please other people. Quite literally, "they" won't let

---

[1]Cf. also Eric Voegelin, *Science, Politics & Gnosticism*, Gateway ed. (Washington, D.C.: Regnery, 1997).

us be good, so we've got to get ourselves "back" to the garden by moving ahead into our progressing world of freer self-expression, freed from the need to flatter the opinions of others.

Ironically, what allows us the ability to pursue this freedom is our liberation from the constraints of nature accomplished already by our fall into the manipulative power of knowledge. This is why we must still work during the week. On weekends, however, the more progressive manipulation of our very selves through mind-altering drugs, drink, birth control, silicone and latex, coupled with the poetic creation of new worlds on TV and the movies, allows us to live the illusion of a nonfallen world where we all do "just get along" because we are too well-entertained to cause any trouble. We are just as selfish as before and still think only of ourselves, but now other people do not torment us with their threatening moves or threatening looks because the sting has been taken out of our thumotic tendencies through a surfeit of erotic satisfaction.

Or has it? Do we not want something more? Do we still not want to admire ourselves? To be worthy of honor? To not just feel good but also actually know we *are* good? As much as we may be erotically satisfied or erotically distracted, what still remains is the thumotic desire to be proud of ourselves with that pride grounded in genuine knowledge. If we truly do want that, if we truly do want pride grounded in knowledge, we must turn to an older and more traditional account of our fall. We must turn to the earlier account of the Fall that the Romantic Fall was designed to replace.

For in this account alone is our loss of knowledge a great evil and ruin, and the regaining of knowledge a great benefit and greatly to be desired. In this account alone do we reckon with a wickedness and evil that is in ourselves, manifest in our deceitful desire to blame others. And in this account alone is knowledge our friend, designed for our good even as it now co-conspires in our loss. Above all, in this account alone can we glimpse the missing element in our erotic and thumotic selves that can bring them to heel and make of us an integral whole—a whole that can pursue its own good with that good preeminently shareable and at one with everyone else's good with no need to hide our desires or allay our fears. For any account of a fall that does not go back to the root and demand a radical solution to a radical problem is doing no more than trafficking in lies; and lies are our problem, not our cure. Let us return, then, to the earlier story and see how all this lying got its start.

In the Bible, the story of the Fall is preceded by God's act of creation that follows a distinctive pattern. "And God said 'Let there be light'; and there was light. And God saw that the light was good" (Genesis 1:3). In this, the first mention of goodness, God first speaks and thinks something, brings it into existence, and then evaluates it as good because he "sees" that what now exists corresponds to its thought or idea. Like an architect who sees that his building corresponds to its blueprints, the goodness he sees is not in the architect or the blueprints, but in the actual building itself.

Consider for a moment an opposite situation. A self-expressive artist throws paint against a white canvas out of anger. He pronounces it good. Why? Because he has expressed himself. The goodness is found in the artist himself, for what he sees is himself and his anger on the canvas. If you had a world created by this sort of god, you would find in the beginning not the

---

It says: "In the beginning was the *Word*."

Already I am stopped. It seems absurd.

The *Word* does not deserve the highest prize,

I must translate it otherwise

If I am well inspired and not blind.

It says: In the beginning was the *Mind*.

Ponder that first line, wait and see,

Lest you should write too hastily.

Is mind the all creating source?

It ought to say: In the beginning there was a *Force*.

Yet something warns me as I grasp the pen,

That my translation must be changed again.

The spirit helps me. Now it is exact.

　　I write: In the beginning was the *Act*.

*Goethe,* Faust, *part 1, 1224-1237*

---

"word" or idea, but the "deed" itself of merely making or expressing.

Such a world would be good because it is an extension of the creator, and this creator would be loving only himself and his own. Like parents who love their own children merely because they are their own, such love needs no knowledge, but only possession and desire. In the beginning of the Bible this is *not* what we are initially dealing with, but we soon will.

After creating everything and seeing that it is "very good," God places Adam and Eve in a garden with two trees, the tree of life and the tree of the knowledge of good and evil. Adam and Eve are initially described as "one flesh," and, because of this shareability, "were both naked, and were not ashamed" (Genesis 2:24-25). Adam was allowed to eat of any tree in the garden but one—the tree of the knowledge of good and evil: "for in the day that you eat of it you shall die" (Genesis 2:17). Presumably Adam passes this prohibition on to Eve, for we soon find her speaking with the serpent, the subtlest creature in God's creation, and his subtlety is evidenced as follows: "You will not die; for God knows that when you eat of it your eyes will be opened, and you will be like God, knowing good and evil" (Genesis 3:4-5). Upon hearing these words, words that pit God as a rival jealous of his prerogatives, particularly the ability to know good and evil, Eve takes a new look at this tree. At first she sees nothing she presumably could not have seen before, for she sees that "the tree was good for food, and that it was a delight to the eyes." But then she sees something new, something that comes not from her eyes or her appetite, but from the words of the serpent: "that the tree was to be desired to make one wise" (Genesis 3:6).

With this new bit of "knowledge" we see the first lie, the lie of the serpent who will later be described by Jesus as the devil who has been a murderer from the beginning and "the father of lies" (John 8:44). To see what Jesus is getting at we must work backwards and ask ourselves, what exactly does Adam get when Eve and then he eat of this fruit? Wisdom? An initiation into knowledge out of ignorance? Not quite. Instead, what they see when their "eyes are opened" is that they are naked and now ashamed of that fact. For the first thing they do upon seeing this "new" nakedness is sew together fig leaves to cover themselves. Whatever they see causes them to blush, as it were, but what is there to blush about? What have they seen that must now be covered? Were their private parts intrinsically shameful and evil before and are they just now coming to know it? If so, then God would have created something within his creation that was evil, but he has pronounced it in detail and in its totality as "very good" (Genesis 1:31). Eve already knows this good, for she has already seen that this tree is "good" for food. If it is not the mere fact of their nudity, then, what do Adam and Eve now "know" that makes them ashamed? What is this new "knowledge" they now have?

The one thing new here is not knowledge at all: instead it is the newness of the serpent's temptation itself—"you will be like God"—and the equation of being godlike with being wise. Yet given the way of knowing goodness we have already seen when God "saw" that his creation was good, how could a creature ever know goodness in such a way? A creature could not evaluate what *is* in the light of what is in its own mind; it would have to evaluate what *is* in light of what was in the Creator's mind. Or to put this in terms of desire, how could a creature of eros, thumos and logos, know what is truly desirable without happily imitating the one overarching model, God, who in creating every creature can show what is truly worth wanting? In short, a mere creature must come to know the goodness of what *is* through the Creator. The newness, and the lying impossibility of the serpent's temptation, is to know the good through ourselves as if we were reality's creators, as though we could desire independently of our model—"like God." But neither Adam and Eve, nor the serpent, nor ourselves, are God—so how can this be done?

To know "like" God knows while not being gods would be to "know" something as good because it is our own, or an extension of our own, like property. It would be to desire as if our desires were our own, free and independent of our model who alone can give them to us. As we saw in the case of artistic self-expression, to know the good "like God" is to know and see the goodness only of oneself. We cannot see and know the goodness of things as they are unless we first take them into ourselves and make them our own, hiding from ourselves (as we shall see, violently) the fact their goodness always comes from without.

What then do Adam and Eve see when their eyes are opened? Privacy itself. Their private parts, as their desires, are now strictly their own. They cannot be shared in common, cannot be "one flesh" because they can only see the goodness of the other if it is owned and desired as an extension of their private selves. What they therefore "know" is not goodness, for that has been lost to sight. Instead, what they now "know" is evil, and the new-ness of that evil is the need to dissemble and appear "as" good by hiding the rivalry that now lies at the root of everything they now truly are. The tree of the knowledge of good and evil has yielded knowledge only of the appearances of good, a good that is only good if it is partially covered. In short, they have *fallen into the need to lie.*

When God shows up in the garden, Adam and Eve hide from him, and when God asks why, Adam answers by saying "I was afraid, because I was naked." "Who told you that you were naked?" the Lord asks rhetori-cally. Who indeed, but themselves? They are now naked before the world in their incestual desire to swallow it up as their own, and the threat that desire poses cuts one off from everything and everyone else if it cannot be hidden. They have not gained the knowledge of good and evil, but they have become afraid and cunning, as cunning as the serpent who must lie to survive in a world that one wants to be one's own, but knows it is not.

But that is not all. Adam and Eve gained the knowledge of the need to lie, but they need to lie because they have become essentially murderers. Their private fears and private desires to be like God must will the de-struction of everyone else as rivals standing in the way of those satisfying those desires. If this seems overwrought, consider this odd detail. Upon discovering their nakedness, Adam and Eve sew fig leaves to make aprons to cover themselves. After God has found them out and pronounced his curses, he covers them with animal skins instead of fig leaves. Why? To do so he must kill an animal, shed blood. Something has indeed died on the day Adam and Eve ate of the tree, but the only actual death has been that of an animal other than themselves. Why this mercy, if mercy it in-deed was? Humans were vegetarians up to this point and would remain so until after the flood (cf. Genesis 9:2-6). Why would God then slay an animal to cover their nakedness when pacific fig leaves would serve that purpose just as well?

We must read on, keeping this detail in mind as we proceed to the story about their offspring. Like the House of Atreus, the full flowering of the parent's crime will come out in the children. Note the respective professions of Adam and Eve's first two sons. Cain is a farmer who tills the soil, while Abel is a shepherd who tends sheep. Cain somehow gets it into his head that he will please God by bringing him a sacrifice of his grain. Abel follows suit, only he offers up his "the firstlings of his flock, their fat portions" (Genesis 4:4), which indicates he must shed blood to make his sacrifice. The Lord had regard for Abel's bloody sacrifice, but not for Cain's.

Again, why? It doesn't say. We are left to wonder, but we are left with some obvious clues. After the Lord shows his regard for Abel's sacrifice, "Cain was very angry, and his countenance fell" (Genesis 4:5). Cain's thumotic rivalry is in play, and God notifies him—and us—that this is sin in its purest form. Cain has ideas of what should or should not be regarded, he has his knowledge of good and evil, right and wrong—and the Lord has disagreed! What does he know! Cain is indignant, he is angry at the Creator's justice and would not only prefer his own notions of justice, but would destroy whatever and whoever gets in the way of his notions. God he cannot slay, but he *can* slay his brother, the new object of his free-floating righteous wrath. When they are alone and hidden out in the fields, Cain murders his brother.

The fact that Cain tries to hide this murder reminds us again that the attempt to cover over reveals what must be hidden. Cain is a murderer. Murder and our aptness to murder must be hidden if one is to coexist with others. But if the blood itself cries out from the ground, then blood would seem to reveal our truth. Now we can see why the Lord had regard for Abel's sacrifice and why he covered Adam and Eve in the skins of animals. Blood must be shed to remind us what we are covering up and hiding from each other. The shock of bloodshed, both of humans and of animals, is the jolt to shake us out of our self-deceit into awareness of how dangerous our secret desires are to everyone else. The privacy of our private self, coupled with our private judgments of good and evil, is the coupling of our erotic desire to swallow up everything else and make it our own with the thumotic violence that would call this desire good and just and kill and destroy anything and anyone who would disagree.

Such desires are unlivable, so if we are to survive them, something must

O Lord, open thou my lips,
    and my mouth shall show forth thy praise
For thou hast no delight in sacrifice;
    were I to give a burnt offering, thou wouldst not be pleased.
The sacrifice acceptable to God is a broken spirit
    a broken and contrite heart, O God, thou wilt not despise.

*Psalm 51:15-17*

die. What dies is an innocent victim, a scapegoat. This scapegoat, human or preferably animal, must die and allow us to deceive ourselves that it is the true object of our wrath. But it surely is not, and the creator God of the Bible arranges all the bloodletting in this story to remind us of that fact. Our true object of wrath is the Lord God himself. From the moment we ate of the tree wanting to know good and evil "like God," what stood in the way of our desire was that very Creator, who, by his very presence and status of making the world a creation that is *not* our own, thwarts us even as he incites us. If we could finally get our hands on him, then, perhaps, we would finally fully see and get what we wanted. Meanwhile, we must live together with all those lesser and yet still competing gods—husbands and wives, brothers and sisters, and all our many neighbors. But how?

The continuing adventures of Cain show us. When Abel's blood cries out from the ground and God describes the result of that cry—that he will now be "cursed from the ground," and that he shall "be a fugitive and a wanderer on the earth" (Genesis 4:10-12)—Cain realizes the implications of this disclosure. "My punishment is greater than I can bear. . . . I shall be a fugitive and a wanderer on the earth, and whoever finds me will slay me" (Genesis 4:13-14). The truth behind the bloody skin-covering of Adam and Eve is now manifest—murderers cannot live with one another. The erotic and thumotic desires leading to our desire to own justice and other bodies, is invariably met with others' erotic fears of losing their bodies and their own thumotic demands for vengeance. With his hidden heart now uncovered through the bloody cry of his actual deed, Cain knows he must now be murdered in turn. The lid is off, and the unending cycle of "just" violence we have seen in the *Oresteia* will result in the inevitable destruction and death of all humanity.

Unless there is a cover-up. Out of God's mercy, there is. But God's cover-up is unlike the cover-ups of Greek tragedy. The biblical cover-ups are designed to be *un-covered*, and, finally, to make manifest what at this point is only partially hidden.

"Not so!" the Lord says, "If any one slays Cain, vengeance shall be taken on him sevenfold" (Genesis 4:15). To signify this threat, a mark is put on Cain's forehead. The mark of Cain is a new covering added to the slain animal skins covering Adam and Eve, and, in both, the actual violence or threat of violence reminds of what lies hidden behind them—murderers who must yet live together.

---

Therefore, where there is no true justice there can be no "association of men united by a common sense of right," and therefore no people answering to the definition of Scipio, or Cicero. And if there is no people then there is no "weal of the people," but some kind of mob, not deserving the name of a people. If, therefore, a commonwealth is the "weal of the people," and if a people does not exist where there is no "association by a common sense of right," and there is no right where there is no justice there is no commonwealth.

*Augustine* City of God, *p. 882*

---

With this mark upon his forehead, Cain founds the first city in the Bible. Politics is revealed for what it is, a pack of hidden murderers and thieves who appear to be law-abiding citizens out of fear rather than desire. Inside the heart of every citizen is a fugitive and wanderer who has no place to lay his head because he has exiled himself from both his fellow man and creation. Outside, that same fugitive is a solid citizen who farms, plays well with others and obeys the law.

The continuing biblical narrative is not taken in by these appearances. In fact, it goes out of its way to reveal them for what they are. It makes plain that "the wickedness of man was great in the earth, and that every imagination of the thoughts of his heart was only evil continually" (Genesis 6:5). Even the flood, apparent attempt to cleanse the earth of the "violence" that fills it through humanity, cannot wash this stain away. Even Noah, righteous in the pattern of Abel, cannot change his heart; he can at best repent of it by making it first known. The first act he performs after the waters recede is to build an altar and offer up a burnt offering. Like Abel he knows it is better to scapegoat an animal than let loose his murderous desires. The Lord is pleased with this minimal self-knowledge, even though the "imagination of man's heart" remains "evil from his youth" (Genesis 8:21).

The biblical story of the Fall is an odd sort of educational project. As opposed to the Romantic version, it is not a story of the loss of innocence and the fall into knowledge. It is rather the story of the fall from knowing good through knowing God, into being able to know only the appearances of good and the somewhat unstable and relative benefits of knowing the evil of our own hearts. To know the good one must know the creator God, and through him be able to know, desire and therefore appreciate the goodness of what is. In the fall *from* this knowledge, and in the fall *into* our need to hide from God and from each other, the only good we now "know" is what might be, what might seem to be, or what we would rather not be (desire, deceit and murder). Nevertheless, the desire to know, which is above all to know and happily imitate God, still remains preeminent, even if only in the loss and absence that accounts for why lying and latent violence are in fact our lot. Wanting to know is not our problem; wanting to own and be right in the absence of true knowledge is. In the absence of that knowledge, we must lie and appear to be as good as possible, if only to survive. Most importantly, however, we must not hide the fact of our need to hide from ourselves. We must uncover, at least to ourselves, the same heart that must remain covered before others. Scapegoating may be essential to our survival, but it is *not* good and it is a lie. It is a lie that we must not forget whenever we see blood and know that our own feet would run quickest to shed it.

What is the good of this biblical self-knowledge? If the story of the biblical Fall, like the argument of this book, is to acquaint us with our desperately wicked heart, what is the point? When Moses will later bring down from Mt. Sinai the commandment against coveting, what good is it when it merely condemns all of us to the invisible and yet inevitable imitative desire to want what we do not have? Or what good will it be when Jesus, in his own Sermon on the Mount, will tell us that in our hearts we are all murderers if we have ever thumotically risen in anger against our brother, or all adulterers if we have erotically looked at any woman with lust? Wouldn't we be better off with the Greek tragedies that give us a peek at these truths but then distract us from them through the dramatic action? Wouldn't we be better off if we changed the story to a Romantic fall wherein benign ignorance of our inner self reigns, and we delude ourselves that evil lies only outside of us in others? Maybe then we would be able to "not worry" about ourselves, and so "be happy" as much as we are able in our tranquilized inner solitude of outward distraction.

---

None is righteous, no not one;

no one understands, no one seeks for God.

All have turned aside, together they have gone wrong;

no one does good, not even one.

Their throat is an open grave,

they use their tongues to deceive.

The venom of asps is under their lips.

Their mouth is full of curses and bitterness.

Their feet are swift to shed blood,

in their paths are ruin and misery,

and the way of peace they do not know,

There is no fear of God before their eyes.

*Romans 3:10-18*

---

Perhaps. The Greek solution of believing in the lies of the poets might well work, if we could still take our own artificial devices seriously. But we don't, and, it seems, no longer can. Self-consciousness and the universal solvent of ironic laughter would seem to be our lot in the modern world.

Consequently, the requisite solution of tragic seriousness will always fail us.[2] Since the ascent of the Christian faith with its Lord who is a confessed innocent victim, we have been unable to spectate at violent scapegoating without knowing it is a lie. Like Dorothy in Oz, we invariably find the mere man behind the curtain of scapegoating solutions.

The Romantic solution attempts to reckon with this. In it there are no corporate solutions, but only corporate problems. Solutions must be found in our inner solitude, so we must find our happiness in our personal and grandiose illusions. But illusions they remain, and the narcotic dreams of inner beatitude will sooner or later dissipate when we are forced to awake through the inevitable encounter with the reality of our own death. And what is that death, but the truth itself in all its multifarious and threatening forms? Yet if there is a solution to the problem and the deception we are to ourselves, it can only be on the path to that truth. We cannot leave off the quest. If there is any hope that we can know—and therefore possibly change—our desperately wicked heart, it must be found in knowing the truth about who we really are.

---

[2]Cf. Patrick Downey, *Serious Comedy: The Philosophical and Theological Significance of Tragic and Comic Writing in the Western Tradition* (New York: Lexington Books, 2000), part 3.

# 7

## CAN WE BE GOOD?

*Christianity is strange; it bids man to recognize that he is vile, and even abominable, and bids him want to be like God. Without such a counterweight, his exaltation would make him horribly vain or his abasement horribly abject.*

PASCAL, *PENSÉES*

Who, indeed, can know the human heart? Even the great philosophers, in their aspiration to know everything, knew they knew themselves least of all in their concrete political and bodily particularity.

Yet what could be more worth knowing, and for the same reason, most tempting to lie about? We might know all there is to know about the na-

---

But I have no time for such things; and the reason, my friend is this. I am still unable, as the Delphic inscription orders, to know myself. . . . Am I a beast more complicated and savage than Typho, or am I a tamer, simpler animal with a share in a divine and gentle nature?

*Plato* Phaedrus *229e-230a*

---

ture of the cosmos, the nature of plants and animals, and the history of how life came to develop and diversify, but when it comes to ourselves all we have of a nature is the "condition" of our own unknowability. Whatever we are, we cannot know ourselves from the outside as a botanist comes to know a plant or a zoologist an animal. Yet if we can't know what we are, how will we ever know what we should be good at being so we can *be* good, rather than pursue the good *things* that invariably fail us? If we look within, as our unique capacity of speech and reason would seem to allow, we all too often discover we are the "lying animal" who must appear differently on the outside in order to continue to be at all. Given our erotic and thumotic fears and desires, our very survival depends upon believing we are much more sociable and safe than we truly are. And that is only on the "corporate" political level. On the personal level, we rarely wake up and face the new day without deceiving ourselves about what all our hustle and bustle is expected to achieve. Nevertheless, we are desperate in our deceit and wickedness precisely because we can't stop wanting the truth and wanting to be better and happier than we are.

Our inside is not our outside; we are wont to blame and fear others for the very things we would do ourselves. And for all the evil we fear and avoid from others, the goods we want rather than the good we might become can only be gained if we become somebody we are not. At best, if we were to tear apart the veils that separate ourselves from each other and ourselves, we might finally see what the underground man of Dostoevsky finally saw, we might say "I" can't be good because of something I have done to myself, rather than deluding myself that "they" won't let me be good. We might. And yet even this hard-won admission seems the most we can know of our own wicked heart.

If so, what is the point? What is the good of such knowledge? If this is the truth, why should we not just feed on dreams? Are we not in the position of Woody Allen's famous joke from *Annie Hall?* "Doc, my brother thinks he is a chicken." "Bring him in, and I'll see what I can do." "Well, I would, except we need the eggs." Needing the eggs of our self-delusion is indeed our problem, but if there is no cure, it remains that without them we will starve.

Historically, with the rise and ascendancy of the philosophical and biblical demand for truthful self-awareness, we can no longer believe the corporate illusions of Greek tragedy. Theatrical blood and violence no longer slake our fearsome blood lust, and the secular political theater of shedding real blood by the bucketful in the trenches and concentration camps of the last century has merely enervated rather than restored us. We are nostalgic for the pagan rites that transformed violence into sacred calm and peace, but all that remains is the ever-increasing need for real and imaginary violence and an ever-receding hope for cathartic release. The comic result of all these tragic attempts to restore meaning and peace is that we immediately see right through them. We cannot overlook the man behind the curtain, and the now chronic ironic laughter at our own expense is small consolation for our inability to take our lives seriously.

Such is our paltry postmodern fate. We see through ourselves and each other like glass, with nothing showing up behind all this transparency. We can laugh at ourselves at each comic exposure of our attempt to hide, but can anything serious come out of such exposure? Can self-knowledge finally lead us somewhere other than to despair? What would it take to become good on the other side of confessing "I can't be good"?

First of all, keep in mind all that we uncovered so far, particularly what we saw in our experiment with the ring of power and invisibility. Recall the narrative accounts of what we found in Greek tragedy and the Bible. Push against the limits of the theoretical life and practical life teased out of Plato and Aristotle. What would it take for us, in all our private fears and desires, to be anything but wicked in our inmost heart? I don't know about you, but for me, it would take a miracle. By a miracle, I mean something we desperately want and need, but something we nonetheless cannot supply through our own resources.

If we could turn away from others, turn towards ourselves and then truly turn out to be good, it would take something radically different than what we now find in ourselves or anyone else. Our erotic fears and desires, not to mention our thumotic fears and desires, only dig us deeper into the hole we are already in. Our desire to know might do us some good, *if* it was our master rather than a useful slave. Yet even if it were, the gap between reason's unlimited reach and its paltry grasp leaves behind what we most need to know—how to solve the concrete problem we are to ourselves. If all the parts of ourselves complemented and reinforced each other, if we were in command of all our faculties, self-knowledge might be worth having. As it is, it seems not. Perhaps on the other side of something miraculously new, it just might be. But should we even hope, much less look for such a miracle? I think we should. Somewhere in the gap between what we need and want and what seems possible, we just might find the most important thing of all.

Let us sketch out what we would need. To begin with our erotic fears and desires, what we need above all else is a *shareable body*. Our particular bodily desires, source of all private property and possession and the fact that what I "have" cannot also be had by another, leads to an overwhelming preponderance of the fear of loss over the desire to have. Even the sexual aspect of eros, the desire for union, intimacy and bodily pleasure with another, is thwarted by that other's ultimately unshareable body. As much as our children might satisfy the desire for two to become one flesh at the biological level, our erotic desire for oneness lies at much higher and deeper levels. Unsated and insatiable, erotic desire in the midst of unshareable bodies leads to the psychological swallowing we see in murder, incest and sadomasochism, all of which seek to transform others into our own private property and flesh. Of course, all such attempts are illusory, and they lead, in one way or another, to the destruction of the other person's body, and, quite often, our own. But when our erotic desires meet our ever-increasing erotic fears, physical or psychological violence inevitably results.

From the simplest things like hunger or poverty, to the most complicated psycho-sexual madnesses of the wealthy with too much time on their hands, our unshareable body is the root of our erotic discontent and human malaise. Whether Plato's noble lie that allows his body politic to appear as a shareable body, or the biblical veil separating Adam's body from Eve's, the appearances and lies that cover our naked unshared bodies with an artificial and fabricated "shareable" body demonstrates just how desperately we are in need of it. And what we most need we can have only in lies and appearances, but not in truth.

At the philosophical level, our unshareable body lies behind the paradoxical "art of dying." If the factual surd at the heart of politics is the human, all-too-human, irrational love of one's own, then to love rationally what is not one's own would be to love no longer the specificity of one's own body or even one's own particular self. To love our specificity as such would be to cut one off from shareable reason, so the philosopher must choose his love. It is that choice that puts him finally at odds with the political, not to mention the familial, in the most profound sense. If, and only if, that particular philosopher's body could be shared, could the philosopher *rationally* love what is his own. Then and only then, could the political cave come out into the light of day, without the artificial illumination of the lies of poetry that are always restricted to the perspective of some one particularity to the violent exclusion of another.

If a truly shareable body is the miracle required at the level of eros, what of thumos? What is required to transform the madness of our ungoverned passion for justice and the glory of being seen and approved of into a salutary service of true justice—with or without applause? What prevents mimetic models from turning into rivals, especially when the vertical ordering needed to prevent this is seen for the lie it must be? Even more, what prevents the inevitable demise of factual virtue as soon as there is no longer a living model and exemplar to get the ball rolling on virtue's circular mimetic process?

What would be required is a particular sort of king—a king who *knows*. As an actor and exemplar such a king bestows on all the possibility of virtue, and as a knower and prince he bestows on us an unshakeable vertical ordering founded upon reality rather than changing social opinion. Reality itself would stand in the way of turning such a model into a rival. This king must provide a true knowledge of justice to satisfy the thumotic longing to serve and fight for justice, even while being able to properly acknowledge this service in the bargain. Above all, however, such a king would have to dispel the mimetic illusion of the guilty victim who provides a delusory sense of justice and ordering through the production of "friends" and "enemies" out of the scapegoating process.

Politically, such a prince would need to overcome the usual covert subordination of thumos to eros that takes place when thumos is willing to fight or die for friends and enemies that are decided not through logos, but through the irrational loyalties generated through erotic belonging and possession. Friends and enemies are, in this sense, an extension of the irrational love of our own to imaginary bodily groups that still essentially require to be distinguished from other bodily groups that are not our "own." Whether clan, city or nation, each requires a mirroring enemy that is not "owned" if they are to harness our thumotic loyalties. For a prince to overcome this he would have to generate genuine friendship based upon knowledge of what is owned by no one but shared in by all. Such friendship would also dispel the illusion of any enemy other than this irrationality itself. Yet if this king is not to lie at this point, as Plato's own philosopher-

---

Hence, it is only proper knowledge of God that fully can meet the question, *quid sit Deus.* But proper knowledge is an act of understanding in virtue of a form proportionate to the object; hence proper knowledge of God must be in virtue of a form an infinite form, in virtue of God himself; such knowledge is beyond the natural proportion of any possible finite substance and so is strictly supernatural; . . . and is identical with the act commonly named the beatific vision. . . . It can be thought only because one has the faith, knows the fact of the beatific vision, and so must accept its possibility. A philosopher operating solely in the light of natural reason could not conceive that we might understand God properly; for understanding God properly is somehow being God; and somehow being infinite. . . . The best that natural reason can attain is the discovery of the paradox that the desire to understand arises naturally, that its object is the transcendental *ens,* and that the proper fulfillment that naturally is attainable is restricted to the proportionate object of the intellect.

Bernard Lonergan, *"The Natural Desire to See God," in* Collection, *pp. 83-84*

---

king reminds us (*Republic* 459c-d), he would require the aforementioned shareable body, in deed and fact rather than imagination.

Such a king or prince therefore could *not* be a philosopher à la Socrates. He cannot be a friend or mere lover of knowing and wisdom. He must, in fact, truly know. He must be wise, and not with the human wisdom of Socrates, who, precisely because he knows he wants to know everything, knows he does not know. Socrates' very humanity guarantees the frustration of this uniquely human desire. This prince must instead be wise in the divine sense. He must know not just this or that, he must know everything, in general and in every concrete specific detail and occurrence. Only in this knowledge of the whole preceding each particular can his knowledge be truly shareable, with no residue or remainder that requires that irrational complement of the lie we see in the political philosophers.

Yet who could know this whole and remain a human being, however much each human being can't help desiring to know this whole?

Nevertheless, it remains that only a human prince who knows this whole could satisfy our thumotic longing to serve order and justice in service to another human being. If this knowledge stayed only in the lap of God and we served some human being who claimed to be this God's prophet, we remain thumotically stuck, with an irrational loyalty to this prophet's revelation who is himself merely thumotic in his trust in God.

Knowing remains a servant and loyalty its master. In such a case there is no distinction between truth and lies because the question itself breaks faith with that loyalty. Our miracle requires something much more than a purported revelation. It requires a king who knows and acts and possesses a body we can all share.

---

SOCRATES: Because we agree that the pious is loved because it is pious, not that it is pious because it is loved, don't we?

EUTHYPHRO: Yes.

SOCRATES: And, further, that the dear-to-the-gods, because it is loved by gods, is dear-to-the-gods by this very fact of being loved, and not that it is loved because it is dear to the gods. . . . But as it is now, you see that the two are opposite, since they are entirely different from each other. For the one, because it is loved, is the sort of thing to be loved; the other, because it is the sort of thing to be loved, is loved.

*Plato* Euthyphro *10e-11a*

---

Such are the contours of the miracle required, but it is, of course, not humanly possible. It is humanly desirable; indeed it seems the one object that corresponds with the totality of our desires to have, to be seen and to know. It is humanly understandable, for it comports with the highest self-understanding of the philosopher. But it is not humanly recognizable apart from somehow sharing in the knowledge of the whole of that very prince. How else could one know the prince is who he must be without already knowing what the prince knows? Yet then we would not need the prince in the first place. So why talk about a miracle all?

Put simply, because the claim is already out there. It is said to have already occurred, in our very own tradition, in our own ongoing history. Yet the miracle of its reception is every bit as miraculous and part and parcel of the prince who is received. The same biblical tradition that has passed on to us and seconded the philosophical knowledge of our wicked heart has also passed on the claim for this most radical and miraculous of cures.

# 8

## THE HEART OF
## CHRISTIAN FAITH

*Love God and do as you please.*

AUGUSTINE OF HIPPO

To recall this claim, we must return to the Bible and continue reading beyond the Fall and the founding of the first city. We must read the Bible as a narrative whole. We must begin with the beginning and the garden in Genesis, and end with the new beginning and a city in Revelation. Between these two we will find a complete story arc with the human heart as a major protagonist. Even if we don't believe a word of it, we must read it and know what it says of who we are, and why it haunts us with the possibility of what we might become.

Recall the flood and the reason the creator God brought forth the raging waters. "The Lord saw that the wickedness of man was great in the earth, and that every imagination of the thoughts of his heart was only evil continually" (Genesis 6:5). Starting explicitly with Noah (although latently present in the "deep" of Genesis 1:2), waters and sea will stand in for the violent and death-dealing imagination of the heart. Floating through those waters in artificial "arks" will stand in for God's merciful sparing and covering. Going under and dying in natural bodies, as we see in baptism, will stand in for a most radical cure. To see where all this is going, the culminating description in the last book in the Bible has this interesting detail: "Then I saw a new heaven and a new earth; for the first heaven and the first earth had passed away, and the sea was no more" (Revelation 21:1). The sea will be no more because the source of the sea's raging, alienating and death-dealing waters—our desperately wicked heart—has been overcome and transformed.

In the meantime, the mercy of God is what allows Noah to float through this "unplumbed, salt, estranging sea" of human violence and deceit.

Even though the rainbow now promises the Lord will no longer destroy humanity because of its wicked heart, the story reminds us that the heart's naked ferocity must still be covered and hidden. Noah plants a vineyard and passes out naked in his drunkenness. When one of his sons mocks and fails to cover his nakedness, Noah curses not that son but his grandson. When the Bible thwarts our readerly anticipations, we should pay close attention. Why is the grandson cursed who did and saw noth-

---

Who ordered, that their longing's fire
Should be, as soon as kindled, cooled?
Who renders vain their deep desire?—
A god, a god their severence ruled!
And bade betwixt their shores to be
The unplumbed, salt, estranging sea.

*Matthew Arnold, "To Marguerite—Continued"*

---

ing? Because covering, since the skins of Adam and Eve, has everything to do with our ability to pass down civilization. Just as we saw in the *Bacchae*, the movement from boys to Men is a delicate business, and the thin veneer of civilization we need to survive depends upon it. Nevertheless, as much as we need sons to become fathers, nowhere in Noah or his sons and grandsons are we yet dealing with genuine rather than apparent virtue.

When the story moves on to Abraham something new happens relative to "civilization." With him begins the development that seeks to uncover rather than cover those appearances. Abraham lives in Ur of the Chaldeans, essentially a city like Cain's wherein appearances rather than reality must reign. Unlike Cain who was truly a fugitive and a wanderer and yet was allowed to appear settled and at peace with his neighbor, Abraham is summoned out of his city and called to wander. Called out of the city to reveal the true antipolitical and murderous nature of the human heart, Abraham is also called out to believe in something entirely new that will be built upon that uncovering and truth. What Abraham is called to believe in, and what makes him the father of faith, is that new life can come out of the dead and sterile human heart. For when Abraham is promised by God that his descendants shall be as the stars in the heaven and the sand on the shore, the salient fact of his wife's sterile and post-menopausal womb renders his faith in that promise a belief in resurrection. Only the creator God who brought forth something out of nothing can bring forth new life out of death.

Lest we forget, the death involved here is not just the death and absence of erotic fertility in Sarah's womb. Even more so, it is the thumotically deceitful and murderous death-dealing at the heart of politics that must murder a victim and lie about its guilt in order to survive. This is why after God has fulfilled his promise erotically and given Sarah an heir, Abraham is still called to sacrifice and "murder" his son Isaac, à la Abel rather than Cain. Tying his son down and raising the knife, Abraham seems willing to do the deed, but the God in whom he believes stops him and supplies a ram in his son's place. What is going on here? If Abraham is praised for his faith in not withholding even his own son, what is the substance of this faith that sets it apart from the determination of Agamemnon to sacrifice his daughter, Iphigenia?

The difference is twofold. In the first place, this story uncovers all scapegoats for what they are, a merciful substitute for human murder. We have already seen this throughout, whether it be the sacrifice of Abel or the bloody skins of Adam and Eve. More importantly, this story brings out the substantial content of Abraham's faith, that the God in whom he believed would still fulfill his promise even if it required bringing his own sacrificed son's body back from the dead.

This, then, is something new. This is not a stopgap, it is not an essential covering over and lie that does not solve or radically change the situation. It is instead a seeing of the problem in all its bloody reality, with the one solution miraculously possible in the face of that truth. Abraham's faith is not the thumotic loyalty of an unquestioning dog who knows nothing and can know nothing of his master's ways. It is instead the faith of one whose eyes are wide open and knows what is required for his master to prove himself a master without lying. It takes a miracle. And Abraham believes in the God who is father of miracles because he is the one creator of the world whereby such miracles can ever occur. Neither of these two "beliefs," whether of the faithful dog or faithful Abraham, are a knowing. But Abraham's faith, at least, must have as its object the One who is and must be in a position to know, whereas Fido's faith merely requires a reward—it therefore devolves into the mere erotic.

Abraham dies and his descendants begin to multiply, until his grandson's sons find refuge in Egypt in order to survive a famine. Joseph, the one among his brothers who survives their rivalry and deceitful murder (Genesis 37), had opened the way to this backhanded rescue and gives the

---

For the law brings wrath, but where there is no law there is no transgression.

That is why it depends on faith, in order that the promise may rest on grace and be guaranteed to all his descendants—not only to the adherents of the law but also to those who share the faith of Abraham, for he is the father of us all, as it is written, "I have made you the father of many nations"—in the presence of the God in whom he believed, who gives life to the dead and calls into existence the things that do not exist.

*Romans 4:15-17*

---

commentary on it that applies to the entire strategy of God's dealing with his people. "As for you, you meant evil against me; but God meant it for good" (Genesis 50:20).

However, since "meaning evil" is the prerogative of every nation, not just the nation of Israel, the Israelites soon find that refuge turning into bondage. A new Pharaoh who no longer remembers the innocence of Joseph now finds his brothers and descendants guilty of threatening Egypt, so he deals "shrewdly" with them in humanity's typical manner—a targeted, scapegoating murder of the newly born Israelite males. One male survives this flood of scapegoating violence, Moses, named after his rescue from the water in his own Noah-like ark built by his Israelite mother. It is this same Moses, who after thumotically murdering and hiding an Egyptian, and then almost doing the same to an Israelite who questions him, must lead his people beyond their bondage by going through the sea and wilderness of his and their own contagious murderousness and deceit. But before leading them across the Red Sea of violent hearts, he must preside over the last and final plague that points ahead to an even greater rescue from bondage.

On the night of Passover, commanded to be commemorated ever after by the Israelites, the logic of scapegoating at the foundation of this and all other nations, along with all its injustice and inadequacy, is made manifest. The angel of death will slay the firstborn of the Egyptians, from Pharaoh down to his maidservant, even to their cattle. Contrarily, if the Israelites sacrifice an unblemished lamb and put its blood on the doorposts and lintel, the angel of death will "pass over" and spare them. Like the actual body of Isaac spared by his substitute ram, here the "corporate" nation of Israel will be spared by a substitute animal. More importantly and to the point, the sacrifice that will allow these people to go free is the substitution of their enemies' firstborn for their own. The blood of animals and humans is conflated, so that the blood of enemies and friends can be separated. What is manifest in all this confusion and separation is that it is all for the sake of avoiding the murderous death we saw at the beginning of Moses' career, the Egyptians' career and the Israelites' career in the common arena of Egypt. Everyone's career seems to "mean evil" because of their various erotic and thumotic fears and desires, and yet God somehow means it all for good. Yet the question must be asked: how can God mean this Passover for good, especially at the price of the Egyptian firstborn? Is God also inescapably involved in the scapegoating business? Or are we to remember this business every year at Passover for a purpose? We must await the full story before we get an answer.

In the meantime, God's chosen people, rescued from the bondage of appearances in Egypt, must wander forty years in the wilderness to manifest (like their common father Abraham), their true status as the wandering, unmarked Cain. In addition to the law of nature condemning them to this wandering (this law was manifest in Abel's blood crying out from the ground), their Lord will now give them his own Law, making even more manifest the thumotic and erotic crimes his mercy has so far covered as much as uncovered.

Freedom and the thumotic concern with modeling, order and rule are now at stake. Israel as a corporate unity is spoken of as the Lord's son, but later it is also spoken of as the Lord's bride and wife. But this erotic bride and thumotic son is in bondage; it is ruled not by what should rule but by what should be ruled. The story of Israel's release from external bondage, along with the giving of the Law on Sinai, reveals plainly that true bondage is internal and involves a disorder wherein what should be ordered rules, and that disloyalty to the true father and Lord is also a whoring after false gods and lies. The principle commandment—that "you shall love the LORD your God with all your heart, and with all your soul, and with all your might" (Deuteronomy 6:5)—brings out the erotic/thumotic blend of this imperative that must love and have for its object of desire the true source of thumotic rule and order.

Nevertheless, this God who has chosen his people is not partial. He is not loyal to his own except insofar as his own realize that they are beholden to everyone who is owned by no one but God. The righteousness of his people will not be judged by how they take care of their own, but how they take care of those who are not owned—the widows, orphans and strangers in their midst, "for you were strangers" in the land of Egypt (Exodus 22:21-24). The heirs of Abraham have no land that is truly their own apart from the Lord who truly owns everything and gives what he gives always on lease. Being called out with Abraham to be strangers in a strange land, the nation of Israel's role is to uncover what is hidden in the false homeyness of cities exemplified by Cain. It is not because of the righteousness of Israel that the Lord is dispossessing the Canaanites; it is because of the Canaanites' heretofore hidden wickedness (Deuteronomy 9:4-5).

What, then, has Israel to offer the nations if it does not have its own righteousness? What it has is the *promise* to Abraham that through this bloodline the need for the covering of blood will cease, that the wicked heart that must now remain covered will then be transformed. Note the injunction: "Circumcise, therefore the foreskin of your heart" (Deuteronomy 10:16). Here is a command no one can fulfill—the bloody circumcision of their own private parts must be transformed into the nonbloody circumcision of their hidden hearts.

In the first king chosen by God rather than by his people, we find that David is "a man after God's own heart" even as he reveals exactly what is hidden in his own (1 Samuel 13:14). For David, when kings should go to war and serve their people, stays home and commits adultery with Bathsheba. Upon finding her pregnant, David has her husband, Uriah—his own loyal subject—murdered. In typical fashion he seeks to cover over his crime, but his Lord will not let him. When the now kingly David pronounces his thumotic condemnation of his own veiled crime—"As the LORD liveth, the man that hath done this thing shall surely die"—Nathan responds, "Thou art the man" (2 Samuel 12:5-7 KJV). Here, in brief, we see the pedagogical function of the Lord's own people before the nations. In our very ire and condemnation of this people who have been given everything and taught everything by the Lord God himself and yet remain stubborn and stiff-necked, we prove that we too have the law and condemn ourselves in our very condemnation of them. "We are the men and women!" whoever we are, for we too are murderers and adulterers. We are unjust in our rule, however small, for we too have disordered the nature of rule internally and externally.

Nevertheless, David remains a man after God's own heart. The one thing needful with hearts as desperately wicked as his and ours is to know them as much as we can, and David knows enough to repent and wait upon the Lord. But what is he waiting for? What new thing can occur when the entire Old Testament seems an intermittent, but slow and steady, descent into the increasing wickedness of God's own people, starting at the top with their own kings? King David is not the last word, just as dead and sterile hearts of stone are not the final fact.

A messiah, a true and just king, must come, even if from the dead, if the promises to Abraham are to be fulfilled. But how could this happen unless God himself, who creates out of nothing and brings life from the dead, does not directly intervene? No longer can he provide a ram or mere covering. Instead, we must uncover completely and yet still deal with the real issue and problem—our hearts are at war with God himself, and if we could, murder him we would.

In its own way, each Gospel in the New Testament begins with a reference to John the Baptist preaching repentance for the forgiveness of sins. Preaching in the wilderness and baptizing in the Jordan, John stands in for the entire project of the Old Testament. In continuity with Adam and Eve's skins, Cain's mark, Noah's ark, Abraham's circumcision, Moses' basket, Israel's Passover and the crossing of the Red Sea, the Ark of the Covenant, and finally, the sacrificial ritual of the high priest once a year

---

And I will give them one heart, and put a new spirit within them; I will take the stony heart out of their flesh and give them a heart of flesh, that they may walk in my statutes and keep my ordinances and obey them; and they shall be my people, and I will be their God.

*Ezekiel 11:19-20*

---

behind the curtain of the temple in the holy of holies, John's baptism represents the artificial and merciful covering over of our murderous desires that (in contradistinction from tragedy) demands repentance rather than a final forgetting of our sin. All of these are "figures" or "types" of the same merciful means of floating across or passing through the sea and wilderness of our murderous hearts ("Yet death reigned from Adam to Moses, even over those whose sins were not like the transgression of Adam, who was a type of the one who was to come" [Romans 5:14]). If the shed blood doesn't remind us, then the dead and drowned Egyptians, not to mention Noah's neighbors, certainly should. John's baptism, however, points ahead to a new baptism qualitatively distinct from his own. "After me comes he who is mightier than I, the thong of whose sandals I am not worthy to stoop down and untie. I have baptized you with water; but he will baptize you with the Holy Spirit" (Mark 1:7-8).

Who must this person be, who no longer just unveils and reminds, but could actually change the bloody murderousness of our hearts? He must have the capacity to create and create anew, and thereby bring life from the dead. Only as a knower of the whole, because he was a creator of the whole, could he rule the thumotically crazed human heart and in so doing subordinate power to knowledge. All four Gospels, each in their own way, must proclaim the good news of God's new creation with a reference to the first beginning of Genesis. For the good news of Jesus, the new and rightful king, is that his right derives from the knowledge he possesses as Creator and hence knower. The gospel according to John couldn't be more explicit about this: "In the beginning was the Word, and the Word was with God, and the Word was God. He was in the beginning with God; all things were made through him, and without him was not anything made that was made. . . . And the Word became flesh and dwelt among us" (John 1:1-3, 14). Only in this case, where the revealer and Lord is fully God and fully man, can the lie built into thumotic loyalty be avoided, for here and only here can one serve knowledge rather than blindly serve power.

No longer is an awareness of the gravity and bloody violent nature of our hearts enough; in the New Testament the emphasis shifts to a complete cure and rebirth of the heart prefigured in the faith of Abraham. For when Jesus arrives (this new Moses become Joshua who does not just glimpse, but will actually lead into the promised land) John the Baptist knows that everything his own baptism represents is not worthy to unlatch the sandals of Jesus' feet. The story must shift from the nation of Israel as the wayward son and faithless bride to Jesus as faithful son, true king, and constant husband and bridegroom. The blending of erotic concern with fidelity and thumotic concern with obedience will come together in Jesus' unique words and deeds. He will be the model and exemplar of a human ordering and ruling over his own soul through what is highest in himself, the knowledge and love of his own and everyone else's Father.

Starting with his own Sermon on the Mount, Jesus fulfills Moses' descent from the mountain by switching the source of authority from the commandments themselves to his own person. "You have heard that it was said to the men of old, 'You shall not kill; and who ever kills shall be liable to judgment.' But I say to you that every one who is angry with his brother shall be liable to judgment" (Matthew 5:21). Likewise, "You have heard that it was said, 'You shall not commit adultery.' But I say to you that every one who looks at a woman lustfully has already committed adultery with her in his heart" (Matthew 5:27-28). Not only is the interior heart emphasized over the exterior deed, but in so doing Jesus is also shifting the emphasis from the commandments that are being violated and the hearts that will continue to do so, to the only one, himself, who can do anything about it.

At the root of all our violations is our mistaken notion of who our enemies are. "You have heard that it was said, 'You shall love your neighbor and hate your enemy.' But I say to you, Love you enemies and pray for those who persecute you" (Matthew 5:43-44). Just as the deeds that violate the commandment are not "out there" in the political world of seeing and being seen, the enemies that will us evil and prevent our good are not "out there" either, causing us to be who we are. Instead, both our enemy *and* the source of our evil is our own wicked and deceitful heart that would know good and evil in the way the serpent said we could, "like God." In our attempt to be like God, not only does God and his created nature become our enemy, but so does everybody else who would be "like God."

Whatever friends we think we have are created out of our fictional distinctions between "my own" and "not my own," which is to say, created with and out of our "enemies." If we are to love reality more than our fictions we must love our enemies even as ourselves. To do this, however, would be to do as the true God and Father does, and do it as creatures rather than the "gods" we flatter ourselves to be. The culmination of Jesus' new commandments is therefore the impossible imperative that we become as he, the most perfect model. "You, therefore, must be perfect, as your heavenly Father is perfect" (Matthew 5:48). To switch from God as our enemy and rival as he is in the garden of Eden to God as our most perfect and loving model, Father and friend, we must get rid of our envious heart with its phony enemies and phony friends and get back to another garden—and it is not the "garden" of Joni Mitchell's Woodstock.

The garden we must get back to is the garden of Gethsemane. It is here that Jesus makes the essential choice and act that brings about a new reality, a new human model and a new human heart. In this garden Jesus might have obeyed his own fears and desires, but he does not. Instead he obeys the desire of his Father who sent him into the world to make this very choice. What Jesus therefore chooses when he cries, "Abba, Father, all things are possible to thee; remove this cup from me; yet not what I will, but what thou wilt" (Mark 14:36), is to obey precisely where Adam disobeyed. Yet what exactly is Jesus choosing, and why must it be here, in a garden? At the Last Supper, on the night of Passover, designed explicitly to recall the passing and nonpassing over of the angel of death, he gives us the crucial words and reason, not to mention an answer to that lingering question—what about the Egyptian firstborn?

For at this supper Jesus breaks a heretofore unshareable loaf of bread and pours each a cup of wine with these words: "This is my body which is given for you. . . . This cup which is poured out for you is the new covenant in my blood" (Luke 22:19-20). Why blood and why his body? Work back from God clothing Adam and Eve in animal skins to their own initial clothing of vegetation. What we arrive at is what caused the need for covering in the first place—Adam's choice. Jesus is about to replay this choice, and his own flesh will play the part of his Eve. Just as Adam's choice cut him off from the flesh he shared with Eve, this second Adam's choice will reunite everyone's sundered flesh in his own body. Nevertheless it is a body that must be broken—murdered and its blood shed. With Jesus' own words as commentary and context, the reason for his arrest, passionate murder and resurrection now become clear.

The context is Adam and Eve's shameful nakedness and Cain's murderousness. In both there is the initial attempt to cover without the shedding of blood, even as God demands a covering requiring bloodshed to remind us of our bloody thoughts and hearts. From God's rejection of Adam and Eve's initial clothing in fig leaves, to the rejection of Cain's sacrifice of grain, God in his seeming bloodthirstiness is actually more concerned with curing us of our own. For when God shows up in the person of his own Son, we will be taught the final lesson about who we are and what we are about. Ever since we heeded the serpent's temptation to be wise "like God" we have wanted to supplant and murder the creator God of the universe. Now, for the first time, we can get our hands on our genuine rival.

In the betrayal and murder of Jesus we can therefore see what is in all our hearts that we must hide from ourselves and each other. Then and only then can we move towards a bloodless cure and a new shareable reality. Now that God has allowed himself to be murdered and we have seen the true intention of our hearts, this voluntary victim in his complete innocence reveals our complete guilt and complicit ignorance in our lies. From his prayer on the cross, "forgive them; for they know not what they do" (Luke 23:34), to the veil in the temple that tears from top to bottom at the moment of his death (Mark 15:38), the murder of Jesus uncovers and reveals the truth behind all our coverings and deceit. We can now know what we are doing and do it no more. Now our shameful need for covering can be safely uncovered, for in the death of this one body alone can we now live with no need to hide.

For if we are to see the truth fully, we must somehow also gain new eyes, new hearts and a new situation that can handle the truth. This new situation arises from the unique nature of this victim. Not only is this victim manifestly innocent and the victimizers guilty, this victim is also God and the Creator himself, who alone can truly know good and evil, and alone can create something entirely new. In addition, as God's own firstborn, "eternally begotten of the Father," Jesus provides the answer to the question hanging since the death of the Egyptian firstborn on the original Passover. Does God's justice rise above the relation of friends and enemies, or is it like all human justice, created out of that distinction? When the Father will send his own firstborn to die for the sake of his enemies, and his son agrees to it, true justice is revealed and the distinction between friends and enemies is overcome. If God will not spare even his own Son in pursuit of a love that will make his enemies into his friends, then in the death and resurrection of this body, slain as a criminal and enemy, can we alone find a truly corporate body politic of justice uniting all in a common amity rather than common enmity.

The miracle of the resurrection of this slain body is therefore the miracle that makes everything else possible. By this body, the body and object of our envy and murderous rivalry, coming back from the dead, we can have a new relation to our own body that can be joined with complete self-knowledge. As we have seen in the classical political philosophers, complete self-knowledge would have to be political knowledge. Yet politics is founded upon a necessary delusion. Here alone, in the kingdom God founded upon the resurrected body of a King crucified outside the walls of a city, could the thumotic and erotic limits of the political be overcome.

The resurrection of Christ's body, for the first time, brings about a truly shareable body and body-politic, which can be seen in the breaking of the now-shareable bread. The communion we can all have in this body makes possible an erotic fulfillment not possible in our situation of unshare-ability and scarcity. For this reason Christ is the bridegroom and his church is both his bride and his own body, the body of Christ. The scarlet whore of unfaithful Israel, who is all of us on our own seeking only our own, is transformed into the virginally pure and white bride who now has everything and is with everyone only through her husband. Erotically, our own insatiability can now be satisfied, and we can as Augustine puts it, "love God and do as we please." For it is through this new shareable body alone that our desires will not find themselves inevitably thwarted.

We also find a new thumotic possibility in Christ's resurrection. For the first time we can have for ourselves a true king. The mimetic nature of our need to serve justice and take pride in how we are seen in the eyes of others can now be met without the violent competition that comes from models that fail us and turn into rivals. If God himself has become man and dwelt among us in such a way that he can be a present and living model to every following generation, we now have an answer to the vicious circle of the virtuous man in Aristotle. If we imitate the virtue of *this* man who because of his resurrection still lives and reigns among us, we can now confidently and truly internalize the prudential quality of his deeds vouchsafed theo-retically by his unique knowledge of the whole as creator.

Not only does Christ provide the concrete possibility of actual virtue grounded theoretically, he also drives out the madness attendant upon our thumotic modeling. Without an agreed upon and stable vertical order, whenever our model gives us an object of desire, the closer that model is to our own level, the more he also gives us a scandal and obstacle to achiev-ing that very same thing. He has become our rival, even as we imitate him as a model. When our model is high above us in order like a king or father he rarely becomes our rival. When he becomes our brother, however, our rivalrous hearts become manifest and the mimetic contagion breaks out that spreads until it takes in even kings and fathers along with all distinguishable ordering. As we saw in Greek tragedy and Cain and Abel, what we need to restore that order is a murder that will prop up a new order on the lie of the "guilty" victim. Hence the foundation of all civilizations is the blood of guilty victims and slain brothers.

So too it might seem with Christ, except that here the lie is made manifest, the victim is innocent and we are guilty. The Father founds his new order on the blood of his innocent Son whom he has not spared (unlike Abraham's son whom the Father did spare) because only this Son's blood could found an order based upon true knowledge and the uncovering of all lies.

The dirty little secret of thumotic chest-thumping that wants to be seen and honored for its willingness to kill and be killed in service to true justice and righteousness is that all this swagger, to its shame, remains in service to veiled erotic fears and desires unless it can gain access to genuine knowledge. Through baptism and the Christian claim to die with Christ and rise again in his new shareable body, we can now thumotically be killed and yet kill the true enemy of justice, the irrational love of our own body. By participating in the one thumotically just deed of Christ's act of obedience to his Father in the Garden of Gethsemane (wherein he agrees to be killed by us and for us on the restored tree of life, the cross) we are now able to do the same by obeying and serving a truly just Father.

Whether this deed is truly just, of course, depends upon who Jesus is and what he knows. For this reason the unique object of Christian faith is Jesus the Christ who must be fully God as much as he is fully man. As a man Christ is a human actor who must act with the same demand for justice as the rest of us, yet as the logos Christ is the knower who knows the whole of justice because he knows the intelligible whole of everything. Christians worthy of the name believe this about Jesus and can be fiercely loyal to the orthodoxy of this "right opinion." Yet as the word *opinion* suggests, how can such believers be anything more than loyal thumotic dogs, like Plato's guardians, who trust this master but never know whether it is the truth or not? Faith is not knowledge, and believing that one's faith is ultimately subordinated to logos does not make it any less thumotic.

Believing remains thumotic through and through and ultimately just as humanly stupid as all our other thumotic madnesses.

Unless, that is, the greatest miracle of all proclaimed in the Christian faith—and the dearest to those philosophically inclined among us—will occur: that we will know him even as we are known. As the apostle Paul puts it, "Now I know in part; then I shall understand fully, even as I have been fully understood" (1 Corinthians 13:12). Here in the Christian hope for cognitive union through love with Christ, otherwise known as the beatific vision, do we find the Christian faith's reckoning with the political problem seen by the political philosophers and proposing the one solution to our seemingly inevitable thumotic illusions.

If, and only if, we could finally know the whole in the way only a Creator of the whole could know it, would our thumos be fully and justly subordinated to a genuine knowledge of justice rather than mere loyalty to God knows what. Only here would we know what God knows; and what the philosopher at least knows he does not know would be taken up into our very self by means of the avowed miracle that by God taking upon himself everything we are, we can take upon ourselves everything he is. Such is the ultimate good news. Only by God himself dwelling among us can he face human wickedness at every level—erotic, thumotic and our desire to know—deal with it as it is, and yet transform it into how we cannot but help think it ought to be.

In short, the good news is that with a full disclosure and knowing of our wicked hearts, we can still hope to become truly good, and not just appear to be good through some sort of obfuscation, abstraction or downright lie. It is a hope; it is the object of faith. But whether or not this faith or hope will prove out is dependent upon whether there is a creator God of this universe who truly loves us, both as we are and how we would want to be.

This is why Christian faith is qualitatively distinct from mere belief, or taking something as true based upon someone else's word. If the object of Christian faith and hope is that Christ is truly the creator Logos of everything, how can one possibly assent to such a thing in the way mere creatures must assent—belief or knowledge? If we could know that Christ is who he says he is, or even know that we should take his word for it, we would already be in possession of the ability to know as God, and so we would have no need of him. To break out of our thumotic limitations we would either already be in possession of knowing as God, however much we may have forgotten that possession, or we would need to receive the condition to know that this man is the creator as much he would have to be the Creator to begin with.

Faith, or the ability to assent to Christ as Lord of all, must be as much a part of the miracle of Christ showing up in the first place. Christian faith is therefore a foretaste of the beatific vision in the most essential sense: it already partakes of the new creation required for us to be capable of truly knowing God as creature, which is to say, only in and through God rather than ourselves.

Christian faith, as opposed to mere belief or thumotic submission, is the heart of flesh and blood resurrected out of our dead and death-dealing hearts of stone. It is the resurrected ability to know how to be truly good. It is the hope that what we now know to do, we can and will. And above

---

Now, if the learner is to obtain the truth, the teacher must bring it to him, but not only that. Along with it, he must provide him with the condition for understanding it, for if the learner were himself the condition for understanding the truth, then he merely needs to recollect, because the condition for understanding the truth is like being able to ask about—the condition and the question contain the conditioned and the answer.

But the one who not only gives the learner the truth but provides the condition is not a teacher. Ultimately, all instruction depends upon the presence of the condition; if it is lacking, then a teacher is capable of nothing, because in the second case, the teacher, before beginning to teach, must transform, not reform, the learner. But no human being is capable of doing this; if it is to take place, it must be done by the god himself.

Søren Kierkegaard, Philosophical Fragments, pp. 14-15

---

all it is the love of the source of goodness in God himself, who gave us the desire for that goodness to begin with, and now allows us to be joined with that source and our end for ever after. Only these three miraculous virtues are fully adequate to the concrete possibility that humans can be virtuous in the ordinary sense of being human in an excellent manner. As we know all too well, it is because we are no good at being ourselves that we are no good at being happy.

Consider, then, the alternatives to this Christian faith. At worst, the insights of the Greek tragedies remain, and we must continue to find a way to hide the truth from ourselves with ever-waning confidence that we will ever succeed. At best, the insights of classical political philosophy will teach us resignation and low expectations in the face of humankind's irremediable thumotic and erotic delusions, consoled by the otherwise intelligible universe. Both alternatives have the same flaw—our desire to know. We cannot help but desire the truth—the whole truth, without a jot or tittle remaining. We spontaneously anticipate the world will make ultimate sense, and because of this anticipation the further question in the face of our wicked hearts is how and why they came to be this way. Even if the world being the way it is leads us to expect no cure, we cannot but ask why it is that way. What *is* in the rest of nature seems like what it *ought* to be, but not with us. What is in us ought not to be. We are excessive, mad, and out of control in our unlimited erotic and thumotic desires. Yet it is this unique excess of our logos that wants to know why this should be the case and why our intelligence and its opening to intelligible reality should want what it cannot have.

Either we cannot make sense of our intelligent desires or we must hope for the beatific vision as the one way we might make complete sense of who we are. Our logos, as weak and quiet a desire as it is amid the din and noise of our other fears and desires, holds the promise that it is the one way our other desires can ever be satisfied. Remaining in all of us, amidst all our wickedness and self-deceit, is the desire to be good because we still want to know what *is*. If we can begin by knowing ourselves, break through our deceit, and confess, "I can't be good," we will then be closer to being good than at any other time in our lives.

All of which is why the Bible, that radical, obnoxious, pervasive, enduring even while hated narrative that makes so much of Western culture what it is, must be listened to and heeded if we are to have any hope that we can come to know who we are and not regret that knowledge. In this book alone do we plunge into the depths of the deceit and violent wickedness lurking in all our hearts—for the sake of and in the hope of transforming those hearts into something radically new and good. This possibility depends, of course, upon whether its account is true—true not only about the good news and promise of Christ's resurrection, but also the wickedness of our own hearts. Without the truth of one the other is a lie.

A common tendency (and the legacy of Romanticism) is to hope for a happy resolution and convenient resurrection, secular or spiritual, even

---

The madman jumped into their midst and pierced them with his eyes. "Whither is God?" he cried; "I will tell you. *We have killed him*—you and I. All of us are his murderers. . . . God is dead. God remains dead. And we have killed him.

How shall we comfort ourselves, the murderers of all murderers? What was holiest and mightiest of all that the world has yet owned has bled to death under our knives; who will wipe this blood off of us? What water is there for us to clean ourselves? What festivals of atonement, what sacred games shall we have to invent? Is not the greatness of this deed too great for us? Must we ourselves not become gods simply to appear worthy of it? There has never been a greater deed; and whoever is born after us—for the sake of this deed he will belong to a higher history than all history hitherto."

*Friedrich Nietzsche,* The Gay Science, *book 3, §123*

---

while denying that our hearts and imaginations are either dead or wicked or generally in need of a resurrection in the first place. Or, perhaps, we may deny the possibility of a resurrection or creator God altogether. Nevertheless, as bleak as our view of human nature in general might be, we don't worry too much about how wicked we ourselves are. Even worse, we might flatter ourselves that we are as philosophically and ironically above it all as the fictional Socrates.

Nietzsche, at least, had this right. If we are to live the life of a philosopher after the advent of Christianity, we must do so self-consciously

---

But why does truth engender hatred? Why does your servant meet with hostility when he preaches the truth, although men love happiness, which is simply the enjoyment of truth? It can only be that man's love of truth is such that when he loves something which is not the truth, he pretends to himself that what he loves is the truth, and because he hates to be proved wrong, he will not allow himself to be convinced he is deceiving himself. So he hates the real truth for the sake of what he takes to his heart in its place.

*Augustine* Confessions *10.23*

---

as an "antichrist" who has the blood of God on his hands and must seek thumotically "to be worthy of such a deed."

Murder and deceit is no longer for those in the cave of politics: it is now at the very heart of who we are as human beings even if it resists being known as our "nature."

Either way, both of these moves involve lying to ourselves. Yet if we think about it (which we don't particularly like to do), every lie is parasitic upon the truth, derives from it and cannot exist without it.

If so, there must be some sort of truth that explains our lying ways, and there would seem to be no better candidate than the story told in the Bible and carried on in the Christian church. Here, and only here, with the greatest hope in the world, can we look ourselves squarely in the eye, see through our appearances and lies, and yet still believe that we can become something new with no need to lie to ourselves or lie before others. If we can believe it, and if it is true, for here the Truth must condition that belief.

Yet what greater need for it to be true can be found than the desperation of our wicked hearts? At the height of our self-knowledge the best we can do is confess with the Underground Man that we cannot be good. How then can we hope to become truly good? Even the biblical story for most of us is a story about how you can please God by forgoing your desires in the short term in order to get the big payoff of heaven in the long term. But by now we should see that this understanding of faith is no more that the civilizing lie of hypocrisy that forgoes what we secretly desire for the sake of gaining wages to be spent elsewhere, or avoiding penalties that we would otherwise predictably suffer. Either way, you are not your own actions, your deeds hide who you really are, and what you consider truly good is *not* what you are doing or who you really are. If this is what the Christian faith consists of, guaranteed, no Christian will ever become good.

But is this common take on these Christian claims at all correct? Have we not read our own habitual hypocrisy into the story, seen it only as the political world writ large, and failed to see through the very lies that this story, with the greatest possible pains, is trying to expose? All the talk of hearts, evil imaginations, bloodshed and violence—talk we tend to over-look as a mere cultural hangover—nevertheless provide the one context in which we can talk about faith, righteousness and heaven without engaging in the very hypocrisy we suppose in everybody but ourselves. This is why the confession of sin, the "I can't be good," must precede everything else. Otherwise, everything else is just plain political and self-medicating BS.

What is the Christian faith, then, if it must always be on the other side of this confession? How can we be good, if we must always keep in mind we cannot? Through that very faith, a faith that is shareably both your own and others'. It is the very same faith as Abraham's who believed new life would come out of the dead womb of his wife, just as he believed his only son, even if murdered, would still rise from the dead to fulfill God's promise. Above all it is the faith of God's own Son whose belief in his own resurrection would be the first act of obedience of an entirely new and shareable body of humanity. The Christian confession is that we have dead hearts, dead to genuine and nonhypocritical goodness, and dead to an ability to live without deceit. Nevertheless, the Christian believes that dead hearts of stone can become alive again, become hearts of flesh and blood, and beat with a genuine desire for goodness and truth.

This is not a wish, a mind-trick, which would make reality conform to what one wants to be. Instead, it is a belief in, a faith in, a particular and unique Person who alone can make such things so. The object of faith is not faith itself, but rather the creator God of the universe, who, as our Father, has raised his incarnate Son from the dead. Faith is only worth as much as its object, the truth of whether or not these things are and whether the event truly happened. We cannot yet know it, which is why we must believe it. Nevertheless, if it has happened, we can see what kind of new goodness and justice it would bring about in ourselves.

It is *not* the apparent goodness we are so used to. On the contrary, it is the goodness that seeks no further reward for being good than that very life of goodness. The inner is the outer and what you see is what you get, for it is a hungering and thirsting for justice that desires nothing else but the satisfaction of its ownmost desire. It is the pleasing of another will who is higher because it is that Will who first gives us our own will. For what this good will wants above all else is to know everything through its source, the God who created everything good, and through that knowledge knows good and evil as a gift rather than a possession. Above all else, what we see is the goodness that would have no enemies but only friends, for goodness that desires only the good has nothing to fear from another but only its own internal injustice. In short, the goodness the Christian believes he can attain is the goodness already manifest in the deeds and actions of Jesus that we hear of in the Gospels.

For at the crucial moment, in Jesus' new garden that will lead to a new city, Adam's act of injustice and disobedience that leads to Cain's city of appearances does *not* occur. In the garden of Gethsemane, Jesus' fear of becoming unjust overcame his fear of suffering an injustice, and the object of Christian faith obeyed the higher in himself and in reality, and so chose to be murdered by his enemies. "For if while we were enemies we were reconciled to God by the death of his Son" (Romans 5:10)—Christian faith believes it will finally have no human enemies other than their old selves who were put to death in that very murder. For not only will Christ's resurrection demonstrate that his body is a shareable one; because it will be the resurrection of the very same body murdered by us as our "enemy," what we can find, to our surprise, is that we have indeed put to death our true enemy, the illusion and deceit of the serpent that puts us at war with everyone and everything, starting with God himself.

If our eyes are opened to that truth, then we can now see with new eyes that Christ's resurrection is also our own into a new life of shareable goodness. Not only will there be no more enemies, but we will be citizens of a city that has a true body politic; for this new city can share in the body of its righteous king as a wife should share in the body of her husband.

> And I saw the holy city, new Jerusalem, coming down out of heaven from God, prepared as a bride adorned for her husband; and I heard a loud voice from the throne saying, "Behold, the dwelling of God is with men. He will dwell with them, and they shall be his people, and God himself will be with them; he will wipe away every tear from their eyes, and death shall be no more, neither shall there be mourning nor crying nor pain any more, for the former things have passed away." (Revelation 21:2-4)

What makes all of this possible is that the desire to know shall be satisfied and we will finally know who we are, what we are doing and what is truly good; for we will know everything there is to know and needed to know to rule ourselves in the light of God's own knowledge of himself. There will no longer be a cave of our own paltry perspectives, for "night shall be no more; they need no light of lamp or sun, for the Lord God will be their light, and they shall reign for ever and ever" (Revelation 22:5). Then, and only then, in the beatific vision, wherein we know everything we have always wanted to know, can we be good, good to our heart's content.

# 9

## BEING GOOD

*Owe no one anything, except to love one another; for he who loves his neighbor has fulfilled the law. The commandments, "You shall not commit adultery, You shall not kill, You shall not steal, You shall not covet," and any other commandment, are summed up in this sentence, "You shall love your neighbor as yourself." Love does no wrong to a neighbor; therefore love is the fulfilling of the law.*

PAUL, THE EPISTLE TO THE ROMANS

If you have come this far in your reading and can truly admit "I can't be good," what then? What can you possibly do about it? Not a thing. But, then again, something can be done. Not by you, but by the One who can alone change such things. In short, a miracle is required, and a miracle of the sort we have just described. So, say you believe in this miracle, again, what then? How does one live out of this miracle and become truly good without the usual appearances and hypocrisies that are only a bit better than being overtly and manifestly wicked? What does being good consist of on the other side of confessing you cannot be good?

As a start remember what precedes that confession: "They won't let me be good." Or as Machiavelli puts it: "For a man who wants to make a profession of good in all regards must come to ruin among so many who are not good."[1] Behind both is the more or less latent fear that if you are

---

[1]Niccolo Machiavelli, *The Prince*, translated and with an introduction by Harvey C. Mansfield (Chicago: University of Chicago Press, 1998), p. 61.

good, "they" will kill you for it, in more ways than one. Exactly. They will. That is step one to becoming good: you must die to the lies, hypocrisies and all-around appearances arising out of your fear of death. Given that you will die, either at the hands of others or mother nature, how can you overcome the seeming necessity of this fear? In the only way possible, by dying with the Lord and Creator of nature, who alone can and promises he will bring us back to life out of that death.

Not only is this the first step in being good, it is also the key to understanding what the good to do and be is. The fear of death motivating Machiavelli's advice and the Underground Man's craven hostility is the shadow cast by the truth that you must die in order to become good. What to them is a threat and "go no further!" argument of necessity is to Christian faith an invitation and promise of an entirely new possibility. To put this another way, the Christian claim that we can only become good by being crucified with Christ is exactly what Machiavelli sees when he says that anyone who wants to be good surrounded by so many who aren't good will come to ruin. It is the same truth, even if seen from an opposite and hostile relationship to the Light that paradoxically illumines that truth. For Machiavelli and the Underground Man, their back is to that light, which is to say, all they know of themselves is the silhouette cast on the screen of their fears. All they know are the others who seem to make them who they are, but they can know nothing of themselves. If they turn around and face their fear of death, they can know themselves in the only way they can be known, in the light of their desires rather than fears. For all their desires, whether the desire to have or the desire to be seen, can only be satisfied and not turn into the shadow of fear in the light of the desire to know who we ourselves are in the light of what continually shines, whether or not we live or die. But if that light is the Light that has come into the world, become flesh, lived and died among us and for us, then we can die and yet live as ourselves out of that self-knowledge (John 1:1-14).

What comes with that self-knowledge is first of all forgiveness. We must forgive others because we ourselves have been forgiven for the wickedness of our own inability to be good. Instead of blaming others for our inability to be good, by forgiving those others we are now free to concentrate on becoming good ourselves no matter the goodness or lack thereof surrounding us. Rather than looking at ourselves through others and then despising them and ourselves for the chains this puts upon us, if we look at others through ourselves as forgiven we are free from them and only beholden to our forgiving and true Lord. This is true freedom *from* others, but the full meaning of this freedom is the freedom *for* others, to love them in the same way we need and want to be loved.

For if there is one short answer to how we can be good after knowing we can't be good, it is that we must love—not just each other, but ourselves and our Lord who first loved us even while we were yet enemies to himself, ourselves and each other. Love is in fact the perfect correlative to self-knowledge, not to mention knowledge in general. Just as the sexual erotic passion that leads us beyond ourselves to unite with another cannot succeed without a shareable third thing, so too the desire to know cannot succeed in unifying with the known without the preexisting united love of God, who as both knower and known conditions the possibility of all knowledge even while providing the desire to know's natural object. This love, that as Dante says in the last line of his *Commedia* "moves the sun and stars," is also the love that moves the still small voice in us that wants to be good in spite of our clamoring fears and lesser desires. Yet because of the intrinsic connection between goodness and knowledge, knowing we can't be good leads us to the true source of our goodness, God.

Love, then, because of its intrinsic combination with forgiveness, is the way for ourselves to be good and yet deal with other people as they are. No matter how tempted we are to look over at others' lack of goodness and know their wickedness in thoroughgoing detail, love demands we know them for what they can become because we know all too well who we are. If the fear of suffering an injustice at their hands no longer motivates our actions, the desire to be just motivates us to know how to do so, and what is required of us is knowledge of our treatment of them, rather than becoming indignant at their treatment of us.

If we lived thus by the golden rule and did unto others as we would have them do unto us, we would have to pay attention to others in a new way. Instead of suspiciously watching out for others as we see our own desires metastasize into a watchful fear of others, a loving desire to satisfy their desires would free us to attend to our own. Since only shareable desires withstand such scrutiny, desire now becomes a passion that unites rather than divides. Love as the cognitive passion par excellence seeks out to know the other's good as one with our own, because being good is essentially knowing the good to do always for ourselves and for our neighbor. Rather than fear being the glue that unites the individuals into a "social contract" even while leaving each member intrinsically and essentially isolated and alone, love is what bonds individuals into a common good.

In a common good rather than a common contract, each individual desires this common good as much as they desire their particular good. Fundamentally, no one can function together without this common good, but as with Machiavelli's inverted advice, our conscious and backwards participation in this good is mediated through our fears rather than desires. When we therefore try to describe it we mistakenly view it as something we make artificially to protect ourselves from each other, rather than something that naturally grows out of our political need for each other. Like Cain, we know we cannot live with our fears, so we cannot help but make an artificial mark that imitates and fakes the common good which we cannot help but desire and truly need. The empty shadow we project unto our commonality and political good is the emptiness of few wanting to be good and many wanting and fearing the loss of good things. Nevertheless, we all still want to be good, which is why we all function, one way or the other, with a common good allowing each one of us to be as good as possible along with everyone else.

Given how obscure the common good is to most of us, the question of what being good would concretely mean for any one of us is a difficult question. What would being good or just look like, especially when so much of what we see of goodness or justice in ourselves and others is done not for its own sake but rather to protect ourselves or get what we want from others? What would our actions look like if we were interested in being good and just, rather than having and keeping good things? Above all, what would our actions look like if we acted out of the love of our Lord who died for us, and so demands that we also prove willing to die for the love of ourselves and each other?

First off, we would have to look at our own body. Locus and fallen source of all other property and possession, our heretofore unshareable body is what leads us into the irrational love of one's own. Now, on the other side of Christ's bodily death and resurrection, shared in through faith and the Eucharist, our body is no longer our own. It has been bought with a price, and the price was the bloodshed our previously mistaken notion of ownership invariably caused. If we are not our own, then neither is our body, and neither is our property. All are now owned by Christ, which is to say, they are all part of the body of Christ, his church and bride. Here, then, we see the intimate connection between sexuality, marriage and the taboo against incest that has dogged the steps of humanity since the Fall. Beginning with baptism that cuts the blood tie with our mother and father, Christians joining in with the death of Christ's body also die to the sexual and tribal connection to unshareable bodies and bodies politic that haunt Greek tragedy. Rising out of the waters of death, rather than merely floating through like Noah's ark, Christians begin a new life as part of a larger shareable body, maintaining both unity and distinction through the head of that body, Christ himself.

What are we to make of the distinctiveness of our own bodies, starting with the distinctiveness of each one of us being either male or female? Is not this font of shareability in the third body of a child also the font of unshareability in the erotic desire between man and woman? Try as we might, we can no longer become the "one flesh" we strive for in the sexual other. If we could consider ourselves as mere biology, this erotic desire would be a neat trick to perpetuate the species, but the insatiability of eros and the incestuous temptation comes not from below but from our severed connection above. In being designed to become one flesh with a man or woman, we see the design to become part of the one flesh of Christ's own body, wherein there is neither male nor female—not because we are lowered below sexual distinction, but because we are raised above and inclusive of it. In one sense there is no male or female in the one flesh of Christ's body ("There is neither Jew nor Greek, there is neither slave nor free, there is neither male nor female; for you are all one in Christ Jesus" [Galatians 3:28]). In another sense there is, for Christ as the head of that body is also the male Bridegroom making the rest of his body his female bride.

This nuptial mystery of the body of Christ, celebrated in the final wedding feast and coronation, is why marriage has such importance in the Christian faith. More than a mere sign of higher things, marriage and the entirety of our erotic desire are how we partake here and now in the shareable body promised through faith. Just as water precedes thirst and the known precedes our desire to know, the final wedding to Christ precedes and accounts for why our erotic expectations so far outstrip our erotic satisfactions.

So again, what would it be like to be good here, in our sexuality, rather

---

And I saw the holy city, new Jerusalem, coming down out of heaven from God, prepared as a bride adorned for her husband.

*Revelation 21:2*


Wives, be subject to your husbands, as to the Lord. For the husband is the head of the wife as Christ is the head of the church, his body, and is himself its Savior. As the church is subject to Christ, so let wives also be subject in everything to their husbands. Husbands, love your wives, as Christ loved the church and gave himself up for her, that he might sanctify her, having cleansed her by the washing of water with the word, that he might present the church to himself in splendor, without spot or wrinkle or any such thing, that she might be holy and without blemish. Even so husbands should love their wives as their own bodies. He who loves his wife loves himself. For no man ever hates his own flesh, but nourishes and cherishes it, as Christ does the church, because we are members of his body. "For this reason a man shall leave his father and mother and be joined to his wife, and the two shall become one flesh." This mystery is a profound one, and I am saying that it refers to Christ and the church; however, let each one of you love his wife as himself, and let the wife see that she respects her husband.

*Ephesians 5:22-33*

---

than our usual trying and failing to have the good things we think we can have? Heck if I know! But I suspect it would be a bit like Joseph in relation to his child, Jesus, and Jesus in relation to his bride, the church. Joseph is merely a ward or steward of the child Jesus who is not his own. Likewise, every baptized child is the same to his own parents. We do not own our children, but rather take care of them in trust until their true Owner comes and expects an accounting. Our relation to our children is thus an extension of our relation to our own body. It is not our own to be used like a tool however we see fit. It has its own ends, determined by its true master who created it and will bring it back from the dead, and we are its steward until the owner regains full possession.

However we treat that body of ours, which we tend to love and nurture spontaneously, is also how we should, if men, treat our wives. Erotically her good would be our own, and we would love her as we love and cherish our own body. Thumotically, however, this would mean a willingness to lay down our life for the benefit of her body rather than our own. Just as ruling as a steward is for the benefit of the ruled, whatever rule a man would have over a woman would be for her benefit rather than his. As a woman, this being ruled can be trusted not as arising from the man himself, but only as vicar or stand-in for her true Lord and ruler, and final husband, Christ, who requires only the obedience he himself models and supplies through his own obedience to the Father in the Garden of Gethsemane. This second Adam will have no veil separating him from his second Eve, the church, because these two will truly and permanently be the one flesh and object of our erotic desire we have had from the beginning.

If this sexual aspect of our erotic madness can only be converted to our good through God's marriage and union with his people, and through our own marriages in God, marriage itself must be seen as a participation in a shareable good that goes beyond our spouses and our children. In a larger and truer sense than the political role of marriage we saw in the *Oresteia*, the sacramental marriage within Christian faith engenders a participation in the political common good without need of the lies and fictions put into the mouth of Apollo and Athena. The transformation of the Furies into the Eumenides, which is to say, the transformation of the privacy of blood ties into the public good of political ties to a body politic, is built into a Christian marriage. Christ as the lamb who was slain is the always-shared-in male husband and father advocated by Apollo. The woman, however, is no longer the chthonic, dark, bloody and unshareable container of the male seed; she is now the virginal, white bride of that lamb whose children will be shared in by everyone who partakes of the same shared body of her husband. This virgin goes far beyond the virgin Athena because she is not the warlike body politic, shared in internally but not externally, but rather the virginal queen, mother and bride who gives birth, marries and rules without need of bloodshed or lies.

If the nuptial mystery at the heart of Christian faith deals with shareability relative to our sexually differentiated bodies, what of property plain and simple? For Marx, the principle solution to all our problems was simple, "Abolition of private property."[2] This has a certain plausibility, especially given the root of so many of our ills in the unshareability of our possessions. In the Marxist view, the privacy of children and women and the troubles that ensue from that privacy are merely an effect of the privacy of property in economic and material relations. How can we be good when we are invariably enmeshed in the tangles of private ownership and private property? Christian believers may view their bodies as owned by and shared in through Christ, yet is that not so much pipe smoke if the property engendered by our economic system is not shared, but is in fact divvied up in an unequal way? In short, will our economic necessities prove shipwreck to all our desires to be good rather than have good things? Will we not need good things of our own in order to survive? And if good things are a necessity, must we not also devise an economic system of communism in order to share in those good things?

As plausible as this might seem as a solution to the problem of our wicked hearts, because it fundamentally requires no change in who we are, it is a further extension of the same problem. Instead of "they" being other people who won't let us be good, the "they" in the case of communism are material economic conditions. Change them, and, presto! We all become good. No self-knowledge or change in one's own self is required. The material condition of history alone is the God who will provide the miracle

---

[2]Karl Marx and Friedrich Engels, *The Communist Manifesto*, ed. Samuel H. Beer (New York: Appleton-Century Crofts, 1955), part 2.

of the shareable bread allowing us to live as new creatures. Apart from the preexisting claim that Christ is also the creator God who can perform such things, of course, no one would think these miraculous claims are even plausible. But if one wants the results of the Christian miracle without needing to believe in Christ, Marxism suits admirably. The price paid is that our problem requiring a miracle is no longer a problem, but then again this miraculous solution is no miracle either.

Nevertheless, the question remains. How can one live out of the miracle of a rebirth of our heart, desire to be good, and yet still take part in an economy based upon private property and legal ownership? Consider again the philosophical description of our problem as "the irrational love of one's own." Imagine what a "rational" love of one's own would look like, particularly when we remind ourselves that we truly own nothing, starting with our "own" body. What a rational or reasonable relation to our body *should* realize is that we no more give our body to ourselves than we can keep it for ourselves. What we can do is deal with it properly while it is here. What then is proper to this body? That we invest in and use this body for the sake of the common good. We should become as good as we can be in the concrete situation we find ourselves in, and so must think through how best to use our own body in order to do so. If our body is as much a charge as our situation, being good requires consideration of how to dispense with what we are given. For who would know better here and now what to do with our situation and body than ourselves?

The same principle holds in the extension of our bodies that we see in our material conditions and private property. Ownership as responsible stewardship extends to private property and makes it the appropriate way to deal with our needed stuff in a rationally attentive way. Paying attention to our stuff, our material conditions, brings out what our stuff is for. It is for others. We receive in order to give. As in the parable of the talents, we have more to give if we rationally invest ourselves in what we have been given.

Private property is the condition for this reinvestment, as long as the privacy here is the mere means to the common destination and good of the giving.

Through baptism we are reminded that our bodies and our children are not our own. Yet who can take better care of our children or our bodies than we ourselves? Are our children then for us? Of course not. They are for the common good, and all partake of the good of new, healthy and well brought-up children. The same is true with our economic "children." All that we have, all that we produce and all that we are paid is the mere means by which we can contribute to the common good. If we think that all our stuff is for us, we are lovers of good things and all our stuff cuts us off from one another. If we are lovers of being good, all our stuff is only a useful way of being good to others. It is indeed better to give than receive, because what we receive is only good for us if it allows us to give and pass along even more. The desire for economic equality is more often than not a desire for equal reception and so robs us of the only true good we can do, which is the goodness of giving. States, bureaucracies, committees and all other sorts of "gatherers and sharers" *give* nothing: only private individuals can give in a way that is good for both giver and receiver. Take away our ability to have and you take away our ability to give.

Being good economically is relatively straightforward. If we are willing to give what we get, the way of sharing built into us as rational creatures

---

For it will be as when a man going on a journey called his servants and entrusted to them his property; to one he gave five talents, to another two, to another one, to each according to is ability. Then he went away. He who had received the five talents went at once and traded with them; and he made five talents more. So also, he who had the two talents made two talents more. But he who had received the one talent went and dug in the ground and hid his master's money. Now after a long time the master of those servants came and settled accounts with them. And he who had received the five talents came forward, bringing five talents more, saying, "Master, you delivered to me five talents, here I have made five talents more." His master said to him, "Well done, good and faithful servant; you have been faithful over a little, I will set you over much; enter into the joy of your master." . . . He also who had received the one talent came forward, saying, "Master, I knew you to be a hard man, reaping where you did not sow, and gathering where you did not winnow; so I was afraid, and I went and hid your talent in the ground. Here you have what is yours." But his master answered him, "You wicked and slothful servant! You knew that I reap where I have not sowed, and gather where I have not winnowed? Then you ought to have invested my money with the bankers, and at my coming I should have received what was my own with interest. So take the talent from him, and give it to him who has the ten talents. For to every one who has will more be given, and he will have abundance; but from him who has not, even what he has will be taken away. And cast the worthless servant into the outer darkness; there men will weep and gnash their teeth."

*Matthew 25:14-21, 24-30*

---

who should be mindful of the true source of increase in our Creator works quite well. Nature is generous under wise stewardship; stingy and recalcitrant under stupid and grasping stewardship. All that we need to do is cultivate our own nature by becoming better at being the rational animal we already are.

Unfortunately, we are not just a rational animal; we are also a political animal, which is to say, thumotic. Here is the true source of scarcity and inequality in human affairs. There seems to be only so much honor and respect to go around. We don't just need to have certain things or get paid a certain amount, we need even more to be seen having those things and being honored by those wages. Of such things there seems a built-in scarcity: if everyone one has them they are not worth having. How are we to *be* good in the thumotic arena of distribution, especially when the desire to be good slips so easily into coveting the praise for being so?

Here is where we must remind ourselves of the doggy nature of thumos. Like Fido, we live for our praise and pats on the back, but they can't come from just anybody, they must come from our master. As much as they seem worthwhile on their own, their true worth comes from an implicit belief about the quality of the master rather than the quantity of the praise. A good master and little praise is better than a bad master and much praise. Alas, as true as that is, dogs and thumos have little discernment and no say in choosing that master. Nevertheless, for humans all genuine thumotic satisfaction depends on having a good one.

Here, then, is the real source of unshareability and scarcity in the realm of thumos. When there is a dispute about the vertical source of honor, the horizontal presence or absence of praise in our packs takes on a life of its own, with each bit of glory containing within itself a phantom father or master. This quarreling among vertically striving brothers, as it were, leads to the unending war and conflict seemingly built into our thumotic nature. All our grasping at dignity and honor can't help but descend into a war over ascendancy, where the desire to receive praise is also a jockeying to be the one in position to give it. The anger and mad-dog quality we most often associate with thumos indicates most of the time our master is defective or absent. A well-trained dog does nothing until the master commands; only then does he act.

In this light, consider the miracle of Christ the King in providing us new hearts whereby we can become good thumotically. If the only true and ultimate master is the source of all our praise and glory, then the usual horizontal scarcity plaguing us means nothing. Praise is worth nothing apart from its vertical source. Likewise, there is no need for the usual struggle for ascendancy because this king and master confirms his rule in the midst of being humiliated and mocked by all the usual sources of putative authority. If this prince's deference and obedience to his Father is the source of his own authority, then he has no need to gain his own by his ascendancy over us or our ascendancy over others.

The source of human dignity is therefore not in the fluctuating horizontal stock market of human recognition; it is now to be found in the vertical image of God built into us from the beginning. To borrow again from the parable of the talents, everybody has been given at least one talent. That minimal talent, the image of God in us, because of its vertical origin in the criteria for all worth, gives each of us our intrinsic worth and dignity as human beings. All further fluctuations, the inevitable more-or-less of further talents given or investments made, lead to no scarcity in praise or glory because their worth derives not from the talent given but the giver who gave it and from our passing on, in turn, of that gift, great or small. The desire to hear, "well done, good and faithful servant" is not covetous because it is shared in vertically by everyone else who has not cut themselves off from that shareable source through their own fear or envy. The wicked servant who buried his one talent is wicked not because of his lacking more talents, but because he feared the loss of even that one. Fear, rather than desire, is the hidden secret behind our coveting.

All of us receive our dignity as a gift, but the reflective source of that dignity in God's own image reminds us of the perils of finding that dignity in the horizontal eyes of one another. Avoiding that peril is perhaps the most important fruit of being good in our thumotic relations with one another. Looking up to see who we are means we do not look side to side except to see how each is made worthy of praise from the same vertical source as ourselves. Not finding our worth in the eyes of others, however, requires a miracle. Absent faith, therefore, there is a tempting solution to our quest for dignity that requires no miracle because it also finds in

---

You are noble, you are rich, you are intelligent and talented, very well, God bless you. I honor you, but I know that I, too, am a man. By honoring you without envy, I show my human dignity before you.

*Fyodor Dostoevsky,* The Brothers Karamazov, *p. 316*

---

ourselves no problem. Like Marx's "solution" in the realm of material relations, this one also is at the level of the "system" rather than ourselves.

The problem is in our organized political relations to other people. We are not free to feel the appropriate sense of honor we think we deserve because the other people surrounding us who could give us that honor take it for themselves and in so doing make us their slaves. It is the conflictual situation we described earlier in the high school experience of "playing chicken." Winners win at the expense of losers, and the dignity and mastery of those few winners is founded upon the humiliation and servitude of the many losers. How do we liberate the many from their bondage? Do we get them to look up to their true master who demands all of us to become a slave of all? That is asking too much! That is asking for miracles!

Instead, what if we arranged our politics in such a way that complete horizontal equality could be achieved? Nobody would be above and nobody would be below. With nobody above us we would be free! How are to do this? By raising everybody up as masters? It cannot be done. All but a few of us swerve in the game of chicken; all of us can't be cool at the same time. What then? Perhaps if we could lower everybody equally to the level of slaves. That is doable, and it sounds so humble and Christian! What then of the masters? If we realize that all of us slaves make them the masters they think they are, making them and us conscious of that illu-

---

"Find a form of association which defends and protects with all common forces the person and goods of each associate, and by means of which each one, while uniting with all, nevertheless obeys only himself and remains as free as before?" This is the fundamental problem for which the social contract provides the solution.

*Jean-Jacques Rousseau,* Social Contract, *1.6*

---

sion, raising awareness of their false consciousness, will make us, in turn, truly the masters. The true master is the horizontal mirroring mass of everybody in general that makes all of us what we are in particular. If we become conscious of this godlike and universal power we have in groups to give ourselves identity, then nobody in particular will be master. Who then will be master? Everybody! The entire realm of our horizontal relations in their totality, internalized in all of us because of our thumotic imitation, will now consciously become the master it already unconsciously was. This "general will" made fully conscious can now be our true master, and all other particular wills must admit to being its slave.

Nevertheless, this servitude is well worth the price as long as no one in particular is master. As long as the winner in the game of chicken is revealed to be the audience to the game and not the one who didn't swerve, all of us get to partake of his courage in the face of death even while remaining the cowards we are in the eyes of each other.

This move, in all its multifarious applications, is the political solution to the problem of thumotic scarcity in our modern world. Some sort of internalized collectivity is alone given mastery. As long as it remains properly general, equal, international and so forth, and as long as it excludes a designated particularity, inequality or nationality, it will liberate us to obey only ourselves (because it is internalized) even at the price of becoming complete slaves to this "general will" of our own social and political creation.

Since this general will must both command and be submitted to, it must take on the vertical quality of a lord and master. It must, in short, function as God. It must be the sort of God who will rescue us from bondage in Egypt, free us from our oppressors through revolution, and give us our Moses in the forms of the totalitarian tyrants who, as embodying the will of the "people," can be safely deified with large posters and statues and microphones. All this talk of freedom and liberation contains within itself the secret of total bondage, and so totalitarian tyranny is not an aberration of the twentieth century, but the inevitable outworking of this serious attempt to overcome thumotic scarcity and meaninglessness.

The idolatry and madness of totalitarianism is easy to see, especially after it has been defeated militarily or economically. What is not so manifest and hence more tempting is the more subtle and insidious forms of the

---

Thus, in order for the social compact to avoid being an empty formula, it tacitly entails the commitment—which alone can give force to the others—that whoever refuses to obey the general will be forced to do so by the entire body. This means merely that he will be forced to be free.

*Jean-Jacques Rousseau,* Social Contract, *1.7*

---

same thing that often pass for mere "morality" rather than politics. From the highest forms of Kantian morality with its "categorical imperative" to our current animus against discrimination between various group identities, the same idolatry of the general and abasement of the particular is usually operative. In Kant, what is moral flows from what can be universalized and demanded of everybody in general. All particular desires are immoral precisely because they are particularly yours. All human dignity, reason and freedom flow from this capacity to universalize; all interests, calculation and servitude flow from our particular egotistical desires. Our thumotic horizontal mirroring is the source of morality if it proves master;

---

But what sort of law can that be the thought of which must determine the will without reference to any expected effect, so that the will can be called absolutely good without qualification? Since I have deprived the will of every impulse that might arise for it from obeying any particular law, there is nothing left to serve the will as principle except the universal conformity of its actions to law as such, i.e., I should never act except in such a way that I can also will that my maxim should become a universal law. Here conformity to law as such (without having as its basis any law determining particular actions) serves the will as principle and must so serve it if duty is not to be a vain delusion and chimerical concept.

*Immanuel Kant,* Metaphysics of Morals, *§1.402*

---

our particular erotic bodily desires are the source of immorality if they do not submit. Imagine the moral as what can be done while holding hands in an unbroken circle, while the immoral is when you step out of the circle and do something on your own.

The call of duty is that the circle may be unbroken. What we have described earlier as bourgeois (when it comes to what we want we think only of ourselves, when it comes to who we are we think only of others), is turned by Kant into the heart of morality. For that very reason, perhaps, most of our moral thinking, when it rises above crude erotic and utilitarian calculation, turns out to be Kantian. Nevertheless, it remains an idolatrous substitution of our horizontal mirroring for a true vertical mastery. It is a solution to our doggy thumotic tendencies devised as if by the dogs themselves, whereby they make the pack itself the master.

Another and more debased form of the same thinking is the moral thinking we do based upon relations between social groups. If some particular social group can be perceived as being oppressed, it will function for all of society as the key to the true consciousness of freedom and morality. False consciousness is on the side of the group that oppresses them. The onlookers and audience to this game of chicken and oppression, especially if they are in the group of the oppressors, must come to the consciousness that the oppressed, the "swervers," are on the side of history, the truth and morality. They are the ones who can transform their oppression to the true liberation of submitting to everybody in general rather than the group of their oppressors in particular. Because of our history of slavery and racism in the United States and the rhetorical similarity to the biblical theme of Exodus, this connection between servitude, liberation, freedom and morality has gained a unique persuasiveness over our imagination. The ease by which we can plug other groups into this moral paradigm, such as women and gays, shows that the true source of its moral force comes not from the Bible but rather from this general secular solution to our thumotic problem. Attaching "ism" after a term such as race or sex is usually a good tip-off that this sort of thinking is at play.

The price we pay for this sort of thumotic solution is that we can no longer be good as individuals, but only in our identification with various groups. As long we are *not* racists, sexists, homophobes or whatever "ists" come next down the pike, we are *eo ipso* good. Even if we have the misfortune of being born as a member of the oppressing majority, as long as we "identify" with the oppressed minority, we are off the hook. We need do or be nothing in particular, but only *have* the appropriate attitude and consciousness of the relations between various social generalities and groups. This sort of morality, to say the least, is all too easy, and the guilt that goes with failing at it is all too facile. We are giving our wicked hearts a pass and plunging further into the depths of our thumotic madness in order to find a cure. It is as if we jumped from a tower to cure our social vertigo.

The larger problem and deadly danger lurking in this morality is that it is a counterfeit deliberately designed to replace Christian faith, the genuine article. It is designed to attain the same end as the promised new heart of Christian faith with no need of a creator god, miracle or resurrection. All that is needed, because it is all we can count on, is the violence and crucifixion at the heart of our thumotic situation. By trading in the talk of liberation from oppression we see in Exodus, by capitalizing on the biblical focus on "strangers" and love of enemies, and by claiming for itself the biblical God's overall plan of bringing good out of evil, the rhetoric of this morality sounds remarkably close to Christian proclamation. But it has all been subtly and deliberately reconstrued.

Beginning with the reinterpretation we saw earlier in the Romantic account of the Fall, the Bible is read as a manifestation and projection of the social and thumotic struggle between human beings upon an imaginary

---

With this, we already have before us the Notion of *Spirit*. What still lies ahead for consciousness is the experience of what Spirit is— this absolute substance which is the unity of the different independent self-consciousnesses which, in their opposition, enjoy perfect freedom and independence: "I" that is "We" and "We" that is "I."

*G. W. F. Hegel,* Phenomenology of Spirit, §177

---

vertical master. The people of God *are* God. Nevertheless, it will require the full working out of the struggle between contending groups to smooth out the various bumps in the circle before the full spiritual equation between the "I" and the "We" can become fully manifest.

That it will work out is the little we need believe; what it truly depends upon is the oldest trick in the book—redirected violence. The thumotic passion to kill or be killed must save us because that is all there is. Logos has been reduced to mere consciousness of the thumotic desire to be recognized. We must crucify in order to be saved, but the victim is no longer the creator God of the universe taking upon himself the sins of his creatures; he is now instead the slaughter bench of history whereupon we will craft our own rivalrous salvation. We will ourselves bring good out of our own evil, even if it will only be at the universal level of history rather than our personal hearts.

If we work back from the contemporary talismanic use of "power" and "struggle" in our moral and political discourse, we can still see how much of our self-understanding depends upon this sort of violence to cure us of our wicked hearts. The hoped-for cure in mass violence is obvious in the right-wing Hegelianism of jack-booted Fascists. Not so obvious is the same hope operative in the violence of revolution and expropriation of the left-wing Hegelians, the Communists. Both came to power after World War I, in which, even at the zenith of bourgeois liberalism, all sides marched off believing in the power of shed blood in renewing and refertilizing the

---

He who dares to undertake the establishment of a people should feel that he is, so to speak, in a position to change human nature, to transform each individual (who by himself is a perfect and solitary whole), into a part of a larger whole from which this individual receives, in a sense, his life and his being; to alter man's constitution in order to strengthen it; to substitute a partial and moral existence for the physical and independent existence we have all received from nature. In a word, he must deny man his own forces in order to give him forces that are alien to him and that he cannot make use of without the help of others. The more these natural forces are dead and obliterated, and the greater and more durable are the acquired forces, the more too is the institution solid and perfect.

*Jean-Jacques Rousseau,* Social Contract, 2.7

---

Western world. Left, right and center, all of educated Europe believed in the power of social violence because of the pseudo-Christian formulations of Hegel, who, in turn, was carrying on the political project of Kant and Rousseau. In their attempt to deal with the political and social problem of thumotic scarcity of meaning in a world of increasing erotic abundance, all placed a foundational act of violence at the center of things. For Rousseau it was the violent and godlike remaking of the lawgiver who would transform human beings from solitary egotists into social beings who live and move and have their being in and through the general will.

The violence involved was that these solitaries must be "forced to be free" by being stripped of their natural liberty and remade into "moral" and "spiritual" citizens who must completely internalize their horizontal bondage and call it "autonomy" and "freedom." What in Rousseau is a historical internalization that makes us "moral" for the first time is in Kant the essential internalization of morality itself. For him the violence is against one's own physical and biological nature, wherein duty and inclination must inevitably and continually conflict, and enjoying one's actions are a sure sign they are immoral. Freud's "discovery" of this unconscious bourgeois dynamite threatening to blow neurotic civilization apart merely uncovers the internalized violence built into this morality. Sadomasochism is an apt description of what happens when internalized society holds the whip over your personal desires in order to gain the feeling of being good.

With Hegel, the use of violence as the means to bring good out of thumotic evil by playing God becomes as obvious and systematic as it can be. Latent and yet increasingly manifest behind his dialectical use of "the negative" and "double negation" is the violent example of the crucifixion, with ourselves doing the crucifying. If you posit something like God at the start, negate that positive (incarnation and crucifixion), you can then negate that negation (resurrection) and come up with something

---

This is the tremendous power of the negative; it is the energy of thought, of the pure "I." Death, if that is what we want to call this non-actuality, is of all things the most dreadful, and to hold fast what is dead requires the greatest strength. . . . But the life of Spirit is not the life that shrinks from death and keeps itself untouched by devastation, but rather the life that endures it and maintains itself in it. It wins its truth only when, in utter dismemberment, it finds itself. . . . Spirit is this power only by looking the negative in the face, and tarrying with it. This tarrying with the negative is the magical power that converts it into being.

G. W. F. Hegel, Phenomenology of Spirit, §32

---

new based entirely on what is latent in the old, that is, the negative and violence.

If you start with isolated egos with their erotic desires as your initial positive, then add thumotic competition between them, you will negate each positive ego through its life-and-death struggle for recognition with everyone else. Nevertheless, once everyone has negated everyone else equally and totally, you will have now negated the negation and are back to a new ego,

---

The *goal,* Absolute Knowing, or Spirit that knows itself as Spirit, has for its part the recollection of the Spirits as they are in themselves and as they accomplish the organization of their realm. Their preservation, regarded from the side of their free existence appearing in the form of contingency, is History; but regarded from the side of their [philosophically] comprehended organization, it is the Science of Knowing in the sphere of appearance: the two together, comprehended History, form alike the inwardizing and the Calvary of absolute Spirit, the actuality, truth, and certainty of his throne, without which he would be lifeless and alone, Only from the chalice of this realm of spirits foams forth for Him his own infinitude.

*G. W. F. Hegel,* Phenomenology of Spirit, *§808*

---

the social "ego" of complete freedom and equality wherein the "I is the We and the We is the I." This new creation Hegel will come right out and call the Spirit in imitation of the Holy Spirit that descends upon the church after the resurrection. For Hegel, humankind itself, through its own historical powers of thumotic violence, will bring itself back from the death of that violence into a new life of spiritual unity. This "speculative Good Friday" and "Calvary of the Absolute Spirit" is for him a theodicy.

Unfortunately, it does not justify God's ways to man, but rather our own historical way of solving the political problem to one another. The good news it preaches is that it is through our own violence, in the aggregate, that we will be saved.

The critique of our thumotic madness and violence in all these thinkers is subtle and profound, so much so that the word *critical* has become in academia a substitute for *philosophical.* Yet all the critique, negativity and violence in the world brings forth nothing positive. They cannot bring about anything truly new because they have no faith in the God who has created everything old. Yet out of that little they must make a crystal palace to live in that rivals the hoped-for kingdom of God. The hidden violence of Greek tragedy and religious ritual that used to found the pagan world of thumotic and political meaning has been blown out of the water through the twin exposures of classical political philosophy and Christian faith. Nevertheless, the need of political foundation remains for those who are neither philosophers in the classical sense nor believers. All that remains are the rear guard actions of these political and theological mystagogues, imitating the God they cannot believe in, even while missing the only thing that can make those ways effective—it is God alone and not ourselves who can re-create out of suffered violence. If we will not allow ourselves to be crucified with Christ, we will only join in by crucifying him and each other.

For Christians, who confess that they cannot be good and yet believe through their Creator's gift in a new and resurrected heart that they *can* be, the challenge is to understand being good politically in the absence of real or apparent enemies. The crucifixion of the Christian God at the hands of his enemies causes immense political and social problems. If we are commanded to love our enemies, the usual foundation of political regimes in enemies who create friends then crumbles—and along with it, a meaningful context for our thumos and its deadly ambitions. Christian faith, in a word, seemed to make violence and politics as we knew it obsolete. Yet our thumos remained. Perhaps, if politics could be founded upon something other than the miraculous "newness" of Christian hearts, politics in the traditional sense might be partially restored.

A first attempt to found politics independent of the destabilizing tendencies of the Christian faith was to argue for a politics based upon purely erotic desires and fears. The fear of suffering death and loss, along with the economic calculation that goes with that fear, was proposed as the new and predictable foundation to replace thumos. Hobbes, Locke and Adam Smith were the great proponents of such a move. Let people operate as much as possible on the base motives of erotic acquisition, and their growing fears and calculations in the aggregate will lead to an "invisible hand" that will accomplish the political ends of corporate unity and structure without anyone intending, planning or ruling it. Such a scheme has the added bonus of working well with Christians who have defused their political passions by loving their enemies, since defeating their enemies economically might not raise the same qualms. Perhaps this is the political solution of Christendom—defuse humanity's thumotic madness through a combination of economic incentives, a base fear of death and loss, and Christian "love" translated à la Locke into toleration.

The fatal flaw in all such schemes is their foundation on such "base" motives. A political structure built upon such low foundations is not as solid as advertised because thumotically we can't help but want to look up to ourselves. If we have nothing worth dying for, we have nothing worth living for, even if we are living in the lap of luxury and peace. Do we have conflict because we want this sort of meaning, or do we need conflict in

---

I esteem Toleration to be the chief
Characteristical Mark of the True Church.

*John Locke,* A Letter Concerning Toleration, *p. 1*

---

order to create this meaning? It is hard to say, but either way the political experiment to found our politics in erotic meaninglessness gave way to the political schemes we have already seen starting with Rousseau. All of them seek essentially a thumotic solution to our political problem, and yet all still had to contend with the Christian demand to love our enemies. What to do? We have already seen the answer: create regimes that seem founded upon the highest moral ground of Christian morality by ostensibly eliminating all enemies through universal freedom and equality, even while retaining the thumotic violence essential to making the regime work.

This, then, is the origin of all the surrogate forms of being good that sound as though they create a new heart for humankind even as they throw us deeper into the thumotic snare that binds us violently to one another. Be it hard core Marxism or the various PC pieties of the cultural Left, all are attempts to provide a political foundation for justice and morality without asking us to stop looking at others to see and become who we are. In fact, they all demand, in one way or the other, that we look at one another to become who we should be. If we don't like what we see, we must change those others by means of a more refined, inclusive and universal political system that will automatically bring us closer to becoming who we want to be. "Social justice" thus becomes a substitute for any one person becoming truly just. A perfect political system of social justice is what being just here would mean, so there will be no thumotic peace until this social justice is attained. All the struggles and more-or-less violent power politics required to achieve this social justice are viewed as a form of pacifism because peace is always its goal no matter how bloody and violent the means. For what is political peace (as we see most clearly in Marx and Hegel) but the complete internalization and universalization of our thumotic competition and violence?

Is this then being good? Is this being just? Is this being truly at peace with one another, much less being at peace with oneself? Of course not. It is a thumotic and political neutering that seeks to obliterate our true desire for the Logos become flesh as master, political king and Prince of Peace. Our thumos knows only that it must look to something beyond itself to find satisfaction, but no matter how we multiply and universalize the thumotic desires of everybody else, thumos remains itself, and this quantification yields no new quality. Like wild dogs in packs we remain masterless, and the worth and meaning of our intrinsic bent towards obedience yields nothing without our proper extrinsic Lord. To become truly good politically and thumotically we are entirely dependent upon what is not thumotic at all, the incarnate wisdom of the universe that all our thumos, both individually and collectively, to its glory, is designed to serve.

If we do serve this Lord, how, then, can we be good? What are Christians to do politically? Can they have enemies? Can they submit to any regime but that of Christ? Can they go to war? Bear arms? Or is pacifism the proper stance of those who serve a Lord who suffers violence but inflicts none? All good and difficult questions. Nevertheless, getting the answers right can be crucial in avoiding the seductive political imitations of Christianity we have already touched on. Just as the question of private property, with all its manifest inequities and problems of unshareability, tempt many to replace the Christian creed with that of Marxism, so too the question of war and the defective justice of political regimes can tempt us to various utopian schemes whose allegiance pulls us away from our final allegiance owed only to the kingdom of God.

For example, take the question of enemies. Since Cain's first city, the friendship between members of a city has been dependent upon fear and hostility toward enemies, whether neighboring tribes, cities, nations or, most elemental of all, the "enemy" we have called the scapegoat. As this scapegoating of enemies reveals, the latent hostility remaining between "friendly" members of a body politic is manifest only against the "enemy." Scare quotes are in order here because of the deep implication of one in the other. The wickedness of our hearts is why this conflict remains, however often it is driven outside the bounds of the city. This is also why justice is only apparent within those bounds. Apparent justice, of course, is better than no justice, but real justice would require real friendship that includes, even as it goes beyond, the law.

How, then, is a Christian to be good in any actual city that derives its justice from its enemies, especially when they are commanded to have no enemies, or, put another way, to love the ones they appear to have? Here, again, is where the imagery of Plato's cave applies. What in the city is only a shadow because friendship is only made through the fiction of enemies (the artificial idol of the scapegoat) is to the Christian believer a natural friendship flowing from its original source in God's love for us. The city knows that this friendship is what it should imitate, so whatever part is lit in the shadow partakes of what a Christian is after directly and wholly. This way of imaging it accounts for why all Christians have viewed themselves as dual citizens—members of the City of God even as they are also members of whatever City of Man they happen here and now to find themselves in. Everything the City of Man needs to function together politically—that is, the appearances of friendship—the Christian already has vis-à-vis his membership in the City of God. Christian citizens, because they are primarily citizens of God's city, the New Jerusalem, are the

> Jesus answered, "My kingship is not of this world; if my kingship
> were of this world, my servants would fight, that I might not be
> handed over to the Jews; but my kingship is not from the world."
> Pilate said to him, "So you are a king?" Jesus answered, "You say
> that I am a king. For this I was born, and for this I have come into
> the world, to bear witness to the truth. Every one who is of the truth
> hears my voice."
>
> *John 18:36-37*

> So Jesus came out, wearing the crown of thorns and the purple
> robe. Pilate said to them, "Behold the man!"
>
> *John 19:5*

best citizens one could possibly have in Cain's sort of city, represented by the old Jerusalem. Even if this city is periodically tempted to crucify those Christians outside the walls of the city as enemies, Christians, like Christ, remain that city's best friend. There was no better friend of the city of Jerusalem than at the moment Christ was being crucified as its enemy, which is why there should be no better friends and citizens in any given city than its Christians (cf. Augustine *City of God*, book 19).

In fact, when Christ stood before Pilate and Pilate spoke of his authority to crucify or release, he confirmed that there was no political authority which was not ultimately to be derived from Christ's own kingdom. While Christ's kingship is not of this world, as the only truly just kingdom, it cannot help but function as the indirect source of all authority in the world.

Crowning Christ with thorns and robing him in purple exemplifies the ironic participation of all apparent justice in the real justice that is its source. When Christ commands us to render unto Caesar the things that are Caesar's, and the things that are God's unto God (Mark 12:17), we must remind ourselves again that neither we nor Caesar own anything that is not given to us: like our talents, everything is on loan. All political regimes are not for themselves, but, like private property, for each other and the common good until they are returned to their true king and master.

Obedience to the laws and statutes of any given city for a Christian is obedience to his or her true lawgiver and judge who puts the law of love above all else.

Love in its connection to knowledge and friendship shows the true origin and fulfillment of every law in the wisdom that promulgates it and the friendship between those who obey it. All politics and lawmaking

---

Let every person be subject to the governing authorities. For there is no authority except from God, and those that exist have been instituted by God. Therefore he who resists the authorities resists what God has appointed, and those who resist will incur judgment. For rulers are not a terror to good conduct, but to bad. Would you have no fear of him who is in authority? Then do what is good, and you will receive his approval, for he is God's servant for your good. But if you do wrong, be afraid, for he does not bear the sword in vain; he is the servant of God to execute his wrath on the wrong-doer. Therefore one must be subject, not only to avoid God's wrath but also for the sake of conscience. For the same reason you also pay taxes, for the authorities are ministers of God, attending to this very thing. Pay all of them their dues, taxes to whom taxes are due, revenue to whom revenue is due, respect to whom respect is due, honor to whom honor is due.

Owe no one anything, except to love one another; for he who loves his neighbor has fulfilled the law. The commandments, "You shall not commit adultery, You shall not kill, You shall not steal, You shall not covet," and any other commandment, are summed up in this sentence, "You shall love your neighbor as yourself." Love does no wrong to a neighbor; therefore love is the fulfilling of the law.

*Romans 13:1-10*

---

within particular regimes, like private property, must be ordered to the common good within that regime. The common good is quite definitely not the general will, because what makes laws just is that they are tied to the goodness between friends rather than the will of hostility against enemies. At the same time, the thumotic temptation of politics, like the temptation of private property, is to view the body politic as something owned by the more thumotic members of that city and useful only as an audience for their needed glory. The common good is then converted into

---

As he entered Capernaum, a centurion came forward to him, beseeching him and saying, "Lord, my servant is lying paralyzed at home, in terrible distress." And he said to him, "I will come and heal him." But the centurion answered him, "Lord, I am not worthy to have you come under my roof; but only say the word, and my servant will be healed. For I am a man under authority, with soldiers under me; and I say to one, 'Go,' and he goes, and to another, 'Come,' and he comes, and to my slave, 'Do this,' and he does it." When Jesus heard him, he marveled, and said to those who followed him, "Truly, I say to you, not even in Israel have I found such faith. I tell you, many will come from east and west and sit at table with Abraham, Isaac, and Jacob in the kingdom of heaven, while the sons of the kingdom will be thrown into the outer darkness; there men will weep and gnash their teeth." And to the centurion Jesus said, "Go; be it done for you as you have believed." And the servant was healed at that very moment.

*Matthew 8:5-13*

---

the particular will of those who must conflict with other wills to achieve that victory and ascendancy. Rule for a Christian in a city cannot be for the glory the city can confer, but only for the glory the kingdom of God can confer. Only with Christ as the ultimate King and vertical source of rank can our thumotic passions be good by serving the common good. When the greatest in Christ's kingdom is the servant of all (Mark 10:42-

45), we see our thumotic passion being addressed in the only way it can be without needing conflict with enemies.

What then of war and soldiers, not to mention policemen and all other occupations in the city that that seem the purest manifestation of thumos in action? Does Christian faith demand the elimination of thumos in actual cities? Is Christian faith a pacifist faith? Is war or even bodily punishment always unjust? As much as these have all been major questions raised within the Christian tradition, the answer has just as traditionally been in the negative. Christian faith is not a pacifist faith. Not only has Christianity had no objection to soldiering per se, Jesus reserves some of his highest words of praise for a Roman centurion, with nary a "go and sin no more" afterwards.

How can this be? Like Pilate who is acknowledged as a representative of legitimate Roman authority even while failing in his use of that authority when he washes his hands, so too are the centurions recognized as performing a legitimate job even while they exploit it by striking and mocking Jesus. What good, then, can possibly come from wielding the

---

"Then it is not the work of the just man to harm either a friend or anyone else, Polemarchus, but of his opposite, the unjust man."

"In my opinion, Socrates," he said, "what you say is entirely true."

"Then if someone asserts that it's just to give what is owed to each man—and he understands by this that harm is owed to enemies by the just man and help to friends—the man who said it was not wise. For he wasn't telling the truth. For it has become apparent to us that it is never just to harm anyone."

*Plato* Republic *335d-e*

---

sword? Is there any possible way to argue that you are not harming but in fact helping those who suffer and are perhaps even killed by that sword?

First of all we must consider what we intend when we treat someone as an enemy rather than a friend. What we intend towards them, because of what we think they intend towards us, is harm. If we are commanded to love these enemies, does that take away their actual or imagined intention to harm? Not at all, but it does take away our intention to harm them. If we love them, not only must we not harm them, we must try to do them a positive good, we must try to benefit them.

Here, then, is an essential insight into our nature gained through thumos. Thumos quite often perceives its good as something that involves pain or even the loss of one's own life. Because we are thumotic, and because thumos seeks to look above rather than below to decide what is good for it, we spontaneously anticipate benefit and harm independent of pleasure and pain and life and death. If we were merely erotic this would

---

I answer that, in order for a war to be just, three things are necessary. First, the authority of the sovereign by whose command the war is to be waged. For it is not the business of a private individual to declare war, because he can seek redress of his rights from the tribunal of his superior. Moreover it is not the business of a private individual to summon together the people, which has to be done in wartime. And as the care of the common weal is committed to those who are in authority, it is their business to watch over the common weal of the city, kingdom or province subject to them. And just as it is lawful for them to have recourse to the sword in defending that common weal against internal disturbances, when they punish evil-doers, according to the words of the Apostle (Romans 13:4): "He beareth not the sword in vain: for he is God's minister, an avenger to execute wrath upon him that doeth evil"; so too, it is their business to have recourse to the sword of war in defending the common weal against external enemies. Hence it is said to those who are in authority (Psalm 81:4): "Rescue the poor: and deliver the needy out of the hand of the sinner"; and for this reason Augustine says (Contra Faust. xxii, 75): "The natural order conducive to peace among mortals demands that the supreme power to declare and counsel war should be in the hands of those who hold supreme authority."

Secondly, a just cause is required, namely that those who are attacked, should be attacked because they deserve it on account of some fault. Wherefore Augustine says (QQ. In Hept., qu. X super Jos.): "A just war is wont to be described as one that avenges wrongs, when a nation or state has to be punished, for refusing to make amends for the wrongs inflicted by its subjects, or to restore what was seized unjustly."

Thirdly, it is necessary that the belligerents should have a rightful intention, so that they intend the advancement of good, or the avoidance of evil. Hence Augustine says (De Verb. Dom.) "True religion looks upon as peaceful those wars that are waged not for motives of aggrandizement, or cruelty, but with the object of securing peace, of punishing evil-doers, and of uplifting the good." For it may happen that the war is declared by the legitimate authority, and for a just cause, and yet be rendered unlawful through a wicked intention. Hence Augustine says (Contra Faust. xxii, 74): "The passion for inflicting harm, the cruel thrist for vengeance, and unpacific and relentless spirit, the fever of revolt, the lust of power, and such like things, all these are rightly condemned in war."

*Thomas Aquinas,* Summa Theologica *II, II q. 40 a. 1*

---

not be the case. But we are not, which means that we are not only capable of determining benefit and harm independent of pleasure and pain, but we are most human when we do so. What this means for war, soldiers and policemen is that it is not only theoretically possible to kill and cause pain even while benefiting those hurt and killed, but it is one of our most distinctively human acts in determining when and how to do so.

The problem with this is obvious. Most of the time thumos intends to harm the recipient of its wrath. It wants vengeance because it perceives its good to be the victim's harm. This, however, is thumos with a defective master. It need not be this way. To use the earlier analogy, a well-trained dog does not bark, bite or move without a nod from its master, and the satisfaction when it does move is not the satisfaction of the bite or bark but the pat of the master. Likewise, the Christian admonition to love even one's enemies is given by the ultimate master of thumos, the incarnate Logos itself, so thumos is now free to find its truest and highest satisfaction in only intending the good of others in all its dealings because of its happy subordination to its natural master.

Nor is this all that surprising. All the time parents find themselves causing pain through punishments to their children, but in all those detentions and spankings, a parent who has overcome their thumotic wrath through love of their children intends nothing but good for them. One can see the same in the case of a good cop. Even if he were to shoot us in the commission of a capital crime, he has given us the good of preventing ourselves from becoming a murderer, or worse, a murderer who gets away with it. If we extend this to cities and nations, the same principle holds, however little it may actually be put in practice. Killing an enemy combatant can be of benefit to that soldier and the nation he militarily represents if his nation's victory would harm both that country and the countries defeated. The military success of Nazi Germany would benefit neither Germany nor the Germans. The death of German soldiers on the battlefield, if it led to their defeat, would benefit both their country and themselves as Germans. For the same reason, the death of noncombatant Germans benefits neither them nor Germany. What is good for them is in fact the only justifiable reason to kill a German soldier.

One could go further in making these distinctions, and what you would have is what has been traditionally codified as "just war" doctrine, a distinctively Christian undertaking that takes seriously the political consequences of Christ's command to love even our enemies. Such thinking may well point out how few wars are truly just, or even provide a handy rationalization of wars undertaken for other reasons, but the mere presence of such a doctrine points out the sort of thinking required for being good even while remaining thumotic and possibly surrounded by others who intend us harm.

As long as our thumos serves its true master, reason, it cannot be harmed, but it can prevent others from harming themselves. As much harm as human thumos causes when running wild and loose, it is nothing in comparison to the good it can achieve when obedient and in service. As every story of heroism in battle or in a fire reminds us, "greater love has no man than this, that a man lay down his life for his friends" (John 15:13). Our hearts beat within us when we hear or sing of such things; what we hear in all such stories is our master's voice, calling us to become good. The master and maker of our human heart, who made us in his own image and likeness, is the same one who promises us new hearts that can hearken to his voice and obey.

Yet he has also promised something even further. Not only can we serve him, and in serving him serve others, we can also go beyond service to something higher and better. We can become his friend. "No longer do I call you servants, for the servant does not know what his master is doing; but I have called you friends, for all that I have heard from my Father I have made known to you" (John 15:15). Politically we know there is something higher than politics. Law, service, justice and obedience are all thumotic; but as thumotic, they go beyond themselves to something higher. That something is friendship with God himself. We are more than dogs who must simply obey. We are human beings whom God, the source of all wisdom and knowledge, has chosen to dwell among as equals. This equality is not the equality that fears domination or submission. It is the equality of love that seeks to know the beloved even as it is known. Of all the desires of our heart, if this desire to know and love God as equals and friends is satisfied, all other desires will be fulfilled. Only then will we be able to love God and do as we please.

# BIBLIOGRAPHY

Aeschylus. *The Eumenides*. In vol. 1 of *Works*. Translated by Richmond Latti-more. Chicago: University of Chicago Press, 1953.

————. *The Oresteia: Agamemnon, The Libation Bearers, The Eumenides*. Trans-lated by Robert Fagles. New York: Viking Press, 1975.

Arnold, Matthew. "To Marguerite—Continued" [1852]. In *A Book of Love Po-etry*. Edited by Jon Stallworthy. New York: Oxford University Press, 1973.

Aristotle. *The Art of Rhetoric*. Translated by Hugh C. Lawson-Tancred. London/New York: Penguin Classics, 1991.

————. *Metaphysics*. A new translation by Joe Sachs. Santa Fe, N.M.: Green Lion Press, 1999.

————. *Nicomachean Ethics*. Translated by Hippocrates G. Apostle. Boston: D. Reidel, 1975.

————. *Nicomachean Ethics*. Translated by Martin Ostwald. New York: Mac-millan/Library of Arts, 1962.

————. *Poetics*. Translated by Hippocrates G. Apostle, Elizabeth A. Dobbs and Morris A. Parslow. Grinnell, Iowa: Peripatetic Press, 1990.

————. *The Politics*. Chicago and London: University of Chicago Press, 1984.

Augustine. *City of God*. Translated by Henry Bettenson. New York: Penguin Books, 1972.

————. *Confessions*. Translated by R. S. Pine-Coffin. London: Penguin Classics, 1961.

Chesterton, G. K. *The Secret of Father Brown*. New York: Penguin Books, 1974.

Dostoevsky, Fyodor. *The Brothers Karamazov*. Translated by Richard Pevear and Larissa Volokhonsky. New York: Vintage, 1991.

Downey, Patrick. *Serious Comedy: The Philosophical and Theological Significance of Tragic and Comic Writing in the Western Tradition*. New York: Lexington Books, 2000.

Euripides. *The Complete Greek Tragedies: Euripides.* Vol. 5: *Electra, The Phoenician Women, The Bacchae.* Chicago: University of Chicago Press, 2002.

Girard, Rene. *I See Satan Fall Like Lightning.* Maryknoll, N.Y.: Orbis, 2001.

Goethe, Johann Wolfgang von. *Faust.* Translated by Walter Kaufmann. New York: Anchor, 1962.

Hegel, G. W. F. *Phenomenology of Spirit.* Translated by A. V. Miller. Oxford: Oxford University Press, 1977.

Heraclitus. Fragment 85, Diels enumeration. Translated by Joe Sachs in *Nicomachean Ethics.* Annapolis, Md.: Focus Publishing, 2002.

Hobbes, Thomas. *De Cive.* New York: Appleton-Century Crofts, 1949.

———. *Leviathan.* New York: Penguin Books, 1968.

Homer. *The Odyssey.* Translated by Robert Fagles. New York: Penguin Books, 1996.

John Paul II. *Evangelium Vitae.* 1995. Available at <www.newadvent.org/library/docs_jp02ev.htm>.

———. *On Social Concern / Sollicitudo Rei Socialis: Encyclical Letter of the Supreme Pontiff John Paul II . . . for the Twentieth Anniversary of Populorum Progresso.* Boston: St. Paul Books & Media, 1987.

Kant, Immanuel. *Grounding for the Metaphysics of Morals, with On a Supposed Right to Lie Because of Philanthropic Concerns.* Indianapolis: Hackett, 1993.

Kierkegaard, Søren. *Philosophical Fragments.* Kierkegaard's Writings 7. Edited and translated by Howard V. Hong and Edna H. Hong. Princeton: Princeton University Press, 1985.

Locke, John. *A Letter Concerning Toleration.* Indianapolis: Hackett, 1983.

———. *The Second Treatise on Government.* Indianapolis: Hackett, 1980.

Lonergan, Bernard. "The Natural Desire to See God." In *Collection,* pp. 83-84. New York: Herder and Herder, 1967.

Machiavelli, Niccolo. *Discourses on Livy.* Translated by Harvey C. Mansfield and Nathan Tarcov. Chicago: University of Chicago Press, 1996.

———. *The Prince.* Translated and with an introduction by Harvey C. Mansfield. Chicago: University of Chicago Press, 1998.

Marx, Karl, and Friedrich Engels. *The Communist Manifesto.* Edited by Samuel H. Beer. New York: Appleton-Century Crofts, 1955.

Nietzsche, Friedrich. *Beyond Good and Evil.* New York: Vintage, 1996.

———. *The Gay Science: With a Prelude in Rhymes and an Appendix of Songs.* New York: Vintage, 1974.

Pascal, Blaise. *Pensées.* Translated by A. J. Krailsheimer. New York: Penguin Classics, 1966.

Plato. *Phaedo.* Translated by David Gallop. New York: Oxford University Press, 1993.

———. *Phaedrus.* Translated by Alexander Nehamas and Paul Woodruff. Indianapolis: Hackett, 1995.

———. *The Republic.* Translated by Allan Bloom. New York: Basic Books, 1991.

———. *Plato's Symposium: A Translation by Seth Benardete with Commentaries by Allan Bloom and Seth Benardete.* Chicago: University of Chicago Press, 2001.

Rousseau, Jean-Jacques. *Basic Political Writings: Discourse on the Sciences and the Arts, Discourse on the Origin of Inequality, Discourse on Political Economy, On the Social Contract.* Translated and edited by Donald A. Cress. Indianapolis: Hackett, 1987.

Schmitt, Carl. *The Concept of the Political.* Translated by George Schwab. Chicago: University of Chicago Press, 1996.

Sophocles. *Oedipus the King.* Translated by David Grene. Chicago: University of Chicago Press, 1991.

Strauss, Leo. *The Rebirth of Classical Political Rationalism: An Introduction to the Thought of Leo Strauss.* Chicago: University of Chicago Press, 1989.

Thomas Aquinas. *Summa Theologica.* Westminster, Md.: Christian Classics, 1948.

Voegelin, Eric. *Science, Politics & Gnosticism.* New York: A Gateway Edition, 1968.

West, Thomas G., and Grace Starry West, trans. *Four Texts on Socrates: Plato's Euthyphro, Apology, and Crito and Aristophanes' Clouds.* Ithaca, N.Y.: Cornell University Press, 1984.

# Subject and Name Index

# Scripture Index